T0013440

A Year and a Day

A Year and a Day

An Experiment in Essays

PHILLIP LOPATE

 New York Review Books New York

This is a New York Review Book

published by The New York Review of Books

207 East 32nd Street, New York, NY 10016

www.nyrb.com

Library of Congress Cataloging-in-Publication Data
Names: Lopate, Phillip, 1943– author.
Title: A year and a day / Phillip Lopate.
Description: New York: New York Review Books, [2023]
Identifiers: LCCN 2023004611 (print) | LCCN 2023004612 (ebook) |
  ISBN 9781681377780 (paperback) | ISBN 9781681377797 (ebook)
Subjects: LCSH: Lopate, Phillip, 1943– | Lopate, Phillip, 1943– —Blogs. |
  American essays—21st century. | Authors, American—21st century—Biography.
Classification: LCC PS3562.O66 Z46 2023 (print) | LCC PS3562.O66 (ebook) |
  DDC 818/.5403—dc23/eng/20230227
LC record available at https://lccn.loc.gov/2023004611
LC ebook record available at https://lccn.loc.gov/2023004612

ISBN 978-1-68137-778-0
Available as an electronic book; ISBN 978-1-68137-779-7

Printed in the United States of America on acid-free paper.

10 9 8 7 6 5 4 3 2 1

Contents

On Keeping a Blog

IN MAY 2016, I contracted to keep a weekly blog for *The American Scholar*. I agreed to write forty-eight entries. Surprisingly, it was more fun than I expected. I had embarked on the project with disdain for the very word *blog*, assuming incorrectly that it was an invitation to sloppy prose and self-involved twaddle. Many blogs are in fact half-baked, but others are elegant and astute, and there is nothing inherently structural about the form that guarantees shoddiness—or quality, for that matter.

I had to overcome an initial dread that I would never be able to meet that weekly deadline over twelve months. I promised myself that in a pinch I could steal from diary entries or reuse old material. I did that only three times. The rest of the year I banged out forty-five individual blog entries, essays, sketches, whatever one chooses to call them.

Were they in fact essays? I'd like to think so, because that would be an incredible feat: writing forty-five new essays in the space of a year. The prose style in the blogs is fairly similar to the one I employ in my essays: the I-character or voice of the narrator, the humor and irony, the attempt to reach some honesty and compositional shapeliness, all basically the same. How could it be otherwise, since I'd trained myself as a personal essayist and at this point in the game could not learn a new "blog style" (if such a thing exists) even if I wanted to. I will say that the prose in these blog pieces is more relaxed and impromptu than in my essay collections, and the endings are often more abrupt than I would have allowed myself in a typical essay. I would come to the end of an idea and think, "Well, it's only a blog; that should be good enough." Originally I was told the blog entries should be between four hundred and one thousand words. Since I almost always went over a thousand words, I figured a rapid closing was legitimate. Leave 'em hungry.

The freedom to exit quickly was only one of the advantages inherent in the form. I also permitted myself to discourse on a range of subjects—books, movies, politics, travel, education, painting, jazz, urban form, past friendships, obituaries, family life—that might have appeared random, presumptuous, or amateurish in another format. I was not putting myself forward as an expert in these matters but only as an observer responding to my latest encounters. In that sense, the blog functioned as a diary. The result, I would like to think, is a self-portrait of one human being's life as it's being lived that is fuller, truer, and more rounded than any I have yet put forth in my previous collections.

The other model I had in mind was *The Pillow Book* by Sei Shonagon. That great catchall of everything and anything has been a temptation to many writers besides myself, who have thought: If only I could find a proper vehicle to deposit all my thoughts in, however trivial. None of us possess Shonagon's tart genius to unify the disparate, but I still always fantasize doing a modern pillow book. This blog experiment is probably the closest I will ever get to it.

Each week I would send in the blog entry to Sudip Bose, my editor at *The American Scholar*, and he would do some light editing, correcting infelicities, while adding an encouraging word, like "wonderful, as always." I doubt he found them equally wonderful, but he was a helpful, tolerant, and reassuring colleague. I needed morale boosting, because from time to time I would panic that I'd never be able to last the full course. Sudip told me I could quit whenever I felt I had run out of gas, which only made me determined to keep at it.

What I discovered was that I could use the blog as a sketchbook. I would sit down at my laptop and verbally doodle a few sentences, and before I knew it I would have the weekly entry roughed out. I would generally wait a day or two before sending it in, and invariably I'd find ways to improve it on the second or third go-round. Having the weekly deadline also gave me the courage to try certain pet ideas that I'd long had in the back of my mind but was, up to then, too frightened to commit to paper—for instance, "On Popularity," "Eros in the Classroom," "To a Passing Stranger"—telling myself it was only a blog, which probably had the most hurried and least demanding of audiences. I could dart in, entertain perverse notions, and then get the hell out before I really get myself in trouble.

It always came as a surprise when someone I knew mentioned that he or she had been enjoying the entries. I had no idea how many "hits" the blog was getting and I did not want to know. It suited me fine to think that no one was reading it, except for a few loyal friends or desperate souls who needed to get a life. Meanwhile, besides keeping a blog, it was a busy year for me: I traveled to China (twice) and India, published a new book, wrote other essays and reviews, taught my classes at Columbia and directed the graduate nonfiction program, went to museums and film festivals, read a lot, and participated in family rituals and quarrels. My daughter graduated from college, moved back in, and got a job, learning certain hard truths about the world of work. The low point in my year, as you might have predicted, was the presidential election, after which I had to wean myself off MSNBC and the nightly news, and not obsess about D—— T——'s latest misbehavior. Some of this got into the blog; some didn't. I did not tell the whole truth or reveal all my secrets. And now that it is done, my most lasting response is one of pure relief: I had dodged a bullet. But I will miss that weekly pat on the head from Sudip, and that momentary euphoria, canceling my panic, when I realized I had figured out what the next week's blog entry would be about.

What follows is not precisely the blog posts as they first appeared. For one thing, I reedited them, making small changes along the way, and the order I assigned them here was at best an approximation of their original chronological sequence. For another, I axed a few that I no longer liked enough to include, and substituted an equal number of short essays I had written since. I have also concluded the book with a longer essay, on experience, as a kind of postscript and demonstration of the way I go about writing more fully developed essays. But the general idea holds: a blog potpourri.

We Begin

I AM STARTING A BLOG, something I thought I would never do. When my late friend Peter M., a worldly man, advised me to keep a blog coincident with the publication of my last book, I pooh-poohed the idea. I also told my publisher's publicist: I don't blog, I don't tweet, I'm not on Facebook, Instagram, MySpace, so you'll just have to promote me without my assisting in these newfangled technical ways. I was playing the geezer card. Never, I thought, would I consent to keep a blog, that catchment for random drivel.

But now I have agreed to write a weekly blog, which is scheduled to run for a year, starting May 2016. Why? Because Sudip Bose, an editor at *The American Scholar* with whom I worked in the past when he was at *Preservation*, asked me to, and I like Sudip, whom I have never met, incidentally, or if I have I don't remember (forgive me, Sudip, it was probably at a crowded literary event), and I'm not even sure if Sudip is a man or a woman, but I think a man—in any case, I've enjoyed the way he dealt with me via emails, and so I agreed. One year, four hundred to one thousand words a week. I am on the road to hell. Or simply, I have finally joined the twenty-first century, sixteen years into it. Good thing I am not a purist. I am an impurist, which is why I voted for Hillary Clinton and not Bernie Sanders in the primary. Oops, there goes half my readership. Well, I've always believed that it's fine for a personal essayist to alienate the reader from time to time, and not insist on warm agreement.

I also thought it might be good to try a blog because it could help generate some unexpected material for future essays, which could then be recycled as *Notes on X*, that sort of thing. Clearly, this first entry will not be useful in that regard. Have I mentioned that the pay for the blog is wretched? I can't wait for Congress to raise the hourly minimum wage. See you next week.

In the meantime, I leave you with a few pointers about my writing process.

I don't write standing up like Hemingway.

I don't write in bed like Proust.

I don't write on Benzedrine like Kerouac.

I don't write in the early hours of the morning like Céline, an insomniac.

I don't write every day like Trollope.

I don't write all dressed up like Keats.

I don't write with the scent of fermenting apples in a nearby drawer, like Schiller.

I don't write agonizingly as if opening a vein, like Ralph Ellison.

I don't write longhand anymore, except in my diaries.

I don't write only when I have inspiration.

I don't write only for money (*pace* Dr. Johnson).

I don't write after sex, though sometimes I turn on the TV and watch the news.

The things I don't write about:

The things I do not write about were one day collecting in my desk and having a conversation. "Hey, why do you think he never writes about us? Is it because we sound funny? No that's not it. Are we too darkly revealing and he's afraid to confess us? Is it because we're too slow that we can't even jump into this fellow's laptop when he turns it on? Is it because we're too dull to be noticed? Too freckled speckled walleyed whatever? Or is it, do you suppose, because we're too important for him to let us into the game this early? He's saving us, that's what!" And so they remained, cheerfully deluded for the rest of their days.

By Way of an Introduction

HELLO, MY NAME IS Phillip Lopate. If you break down these two names, *Phillip* means "lover of horses" and *Lopate* is the word in many Eastern European languages for "shovel," particularly a kind of baker's shovel. As it happens, I have no particular regard for horses; I have ridden horseback only two or three times, and each time I was nervous about being thrown off. I would like to think the name suggests aristocratic lineage, equestrian nobility, that sort of thing, but my great-great-grandfather may have simply been a stable boy. As for shovels, I very rarely have use for one, except during heavy winter snows; and after I turned sixty-five I gave the chore over to my wife, out of fear that I might have a heart attack shoveling (snow is heavier than you may think). What the name *shovel* does suggest is that I am from proletarian stock, which would have been a source of pride had I been living in Soviet Russia or Communist China. But being a United States citizen, I have spent a good part of my life trying to lift myself up from working class to the bourgeoisie.

Hello, my name is Phillip Lopate. In the introduction to my selected essays, *Getting Personal*, I pretended to be a doctor who had come across the manuscript of my friend Phillip Lopate after he died. I had always liked those nineteenth-century novels that began with a preface saying the following papers were found in the board-inghouse of a despondent man who hanged himself—or something like that. It's always fun to play a dying scene; kids do it all the time, stumbling to the ground and clutching their chests as though they'd been shot. Probably it represents the opportunity to surrender to one's self-pity while mocking it. I once made a short film in which I played the hero who died at the end. It was called *The Casserole Dish*.

Anyway, I staged this premature "death" in my book's introduction, and invented a doctor friend who would mourn my passing, calling him Dr. Horst Shovel to give away the joke that it was really me. However, most readers didn't get the allusions, and some of my fans in the hinterlands came to readings advertising my appearance and expressed relief, when I signed their books, that I was still alive on the planet. Someday I will not be around, and then that joke will take on another, more sinister tone. Let us hope not for a long time.

"Hello, my name is Phillip Lopate." I have worn a name tag like this at countless conferences and functions. It always makes me uncomfortable to announce my presence so openly. I prefer to be standoffish; it may surprise you to know that I am really rather shy and reserved. How is it that someone so jealous of his privacy can write brazenly confessional, personal, intimate details about himself? It is a paradox. When I am writing I don't feel shy anymore, I feel like confiding to my ideal, fantasized reader. Montaigne once wrote that things he would be too embarrassed to admit out loud, any stranger might find out by going down to the local bookstore.

Hello, my name is Phillip Lopate. I hope you will enjoy my blog.

A Childhood Comfort Food

KASHA VARNISHKES... the very name brings a smile to my lips, its plethora of shushing sounds invoking silence, simultaneous with its juicy exuberant consonants that demand to be heard. Of course, what delights is not just that onomatopoeic nomenclature (like grains of kasha dissolving in saliva) but the taste-memories lingering from youth.

An oniony dish associated with Russian Jews, though I suspect it may have been eaten by poor Eastern Europeans of all religions, it was prepared by my grandmother on my father's side. Actually, she was my father's stepmother; my grandfather, something of a Bluebeard, buried at least four wives. I myself descend from a mixed marriage (Russian Jewish father and German Jewish mother, talk about your culture clash), and my mother as a rule rarely made these Russian peasant dishes. She didn't despise them, just didn't feel at home making them, so we ate things like stuffed cabbage and borscht at my grandfather's house, or at the many cheap eateries in our neighborhood. We lived in Williamsburg, Brooklyn, when it was still an impoverished ghetto and not a haven for young foodies. As a result, the food was uniformly delicious: At the Sunset Dairy cafeteria, at numerous delicatessens, at the family restaurants like Bella's that welcomed babies by supplying high chairs, you could always get a good kasha varnishkes. A side dish, never the main attraction, but all the more comforting for its humility.

Kasha, let's face it, tastes like nothing, or like nothing with a little dirt thrown in. But once it is *varnished* with onions, chicken fat, and chicken stock, and *garnished* with farfalle (bow tie pasta), it becomes an ideal medium for sopping up flavors. A little salt and pepper will enhance. Some prefer it with brown gravy, but I am a dry kind of guy and would rather take mine straight. You have to coat the kasha with egg first, that's important, because only that will ensure the kasha won't run together in a soggy mush; each grain must retain its own integrity. Think of it as macrobiotic rice, suitable for chewing hundreds of times. Me, I never masticate it more than once or twice, I am too eager to have that semi-piquant, semi-bland (a useful quality in comfort food) union of bow tie pasta, onion, and buckwheat tease my taste buds with each dreamy forkful.

Perhaps the lowly kasha, all too reminiscent of the shtetl, would be appreciated better by Americans if called by its English name, *groat*, an equally strange word, ripe for meditation. Somehow I doubt it. Whenever I start rhapsodizing about this dish, I am told by my wife and daughter that they hate kasha, that it smells like a wet basement and tastes like cardboard. What can you do? They have a right to their (misguided) opinions and I to mine. Each of us is destined to a modicum of isolation in our wayward thoughts, our unappeasable desires, and our nostalgic culinary tastes.

Selling My Papers

THE MOST GRATIFYING EVENT to have occurred this past year—my ambivalence about surrendering them aside—was selling my papers to Yale University's Beinecke Library. The Beinecke is a prestigious repository of many distinguished writers' papers, and to be accepted into that august company must mean I am a distinguished writer, too, no? But it was never a sure thing. Here is how it came about.

For years I had been hearing of people I knew selling their papers, and often these writers were, in my humble judgment, no better practitioners of the literary art than I—indeed, in some cases, inferior! How did they do it? I wondered. I had as yet no urgency to place my papers, still feeling healthy and fit; but in due course I was approached by a bookseller who handled such transactions, which suddenly made it a concrete, attractive possibility. He contacted the New York Public Library, a logical place for my papers given my lifelong involvement with the city of my birth, and two representatives from that estimable institution came to my house to examine the lot. Though I had never been scrupulously anal about archiving myself—one can either live one's life or curate it, not both—I had managed to accumulate quite a heap over the years, simply by tossing papers, drafts, or memorabilia into filing cabinets and closets. In preparation for the librarians' visit I had laid out letters, manuscripts, and diaries on the kitchen table and in boxes all about the room. I tried to steer these two examiners, a man and a woman, to what I thought might be the juiciest bits, but their blank emotionless faces (so like those of foundation heads or oncologists, who don't want to get your hopes up) gave away nothing, and after two hours of idly sifting through the records of a lifetime's labor they departed. Two hours! I had foolishly expected them to take several days to acquaint themselves with my oeuvre, or I should say the documentation surrounding it. I heard nothing back from the NYPL, and eventually had to pry loose from an inside contact that they had decided to pass on my offering. I gather they were going after bigger fish (Tom Wolfe, as it happened).

My first agent, having gotten nowhere at this one attempt, made himself scarcer than a cat burglar and I never heard from him again. A few years passed, and I found another bookseller-agent, who agreed to take me on. We approached Columbia University, an even more logical protector of my effects, since I had been an undergraduate at the school and was now a professor there. Should they decide to purchase my papers, I could be on hand to guide any scholars working on them, to answer questions merely by walking across the quadrangle. A nice young woman came out to my house in Brooklyn, examined the haul for two or three hours (I knew the drill enough not to expect more), and said she would report back to her boss, smiling all the while. Several months passed and again I heard nothing, until finally I phoned the woman and was told that regretfully they had decided to "pass." Why? I demanded, astonished and resentful. This time it was not a matter of snaring bigger fish but of saving money. The budget for acquisitions was very tight, the essay was not going to be one of their areas of concentration, and anyway, they had decided to go with another nonfiction writer whose asking price was cheaper. I also got the impression that since I was an alumnus the thing expected of me was to donate my papers gratis to my alma mater.

By now I had just about given up hope, but my new agent was not dismayed and decided to try Yale. An appointment was arranged for several weeks ahead, giving me enough time to sort through the mounds of papers and distribute them into various piles according to my subspecialties: personal essay, literary criticism, film, architectural and urbanist writings; personal diaries from my teenage years onward; teaching diaries; letters from students, friends, lovers, family members; audiotapes and DVDs of public appearances; novel manuscripts; poetry drafts. . . . I had arranged everything in thirty-six cardboard cartons, with manila folders of correspondence stacked on the kitchen table. My wife thought the handwritten scrawl by which I had marked the boxes' contents with Sharpies was too sloppy. No way, she said, would Yale ever buy my papers unless I relabeled everything neatly, which I refused to do. The night before the librarians from the Beinecke were to arrive, my daughter, taking pity on me, rearranged the boxes as I slept, in what she thought was a more fetching display.

I came downstairs in the morning and inspected the boxy profusion that had taken over the parlor floor. By now I was starting to feel like a garment-center salesman laying out the season's dress line. I knew the spiel and would try to present myself as a Renaissance man, active in various scenes: the open education movement, Writers in the Schools, the New York Film Festival, the resurgent essay, the New York school of poetry scene, the antiwar movement, the Municipal Art Society—if nothing else, a Witness to History. On the one hand, I thought it was a remarkably convincing archive, indisputably valuable to all who cared about belles lettres; on the other hand, I would not have been surprised to be turned down again. Such is the predicament of a midlist writer like myself, respected up to a point but not a Big Name: I could be included in any list or be omitted from it, without raising an eyebrow.

The two women who came to my house seemed well versed in my career and needed little salesmanship. They were both pleasant and upbeat. One of them announced that the Beinecke was looking to strengthen their holdings in creative nonfiction. Vell, ladies, you have come to the rvight place! I cravenly steered them to my pile of letters from Famous People; but one woman, who as luck would have it cared deeply about education, was far less interested in them than in a box of teaching diaries, which she thought fairly rare. The other woman, who specialized in contemporary poetry, noted how many of my correspondents were already in the Beinecke collection, which would make for convenient cross-referencing. After staying three hours they left, intimating that they would make a positive recommendation to purchase the archive at the next meeting. I might have to wait a few months for it to come before the committee, but things looked good. As it happened, I waited only one week before learning they had met my agent's price, which I thought respectable but not asking for the moon.

I now moved all the boxes down to the basement so as to restore the kitchen and living room to normal use. All thirty-six cartons would soon be leaving, bye-bye, my entire past, a life's detritus, the snail's trail of romances and crushes, hopes and betrayals, euphoria and disappointment, the starts of poems that came to nothing, the painstakingly typed and crossed-out prose drafts (precomputer).

I was outsourcing my memory to the Beinecke, and if I ever decided to write my autobiography I would have to go to New Haven and sit in the Yale library, revisiting these diaries and letters. After they had finished cataloging everything they would be happy to make whatever I wanted available on a visit, though I could requisition no more than four files at a time. I could then become a scholar grub, a monk working on the incunabula of my own experience.

I had already made the decision not to hold anything back. It would be madness, I felt, to try to censor potentially harmful passages, whether because they were mean-spiritedly critical of my contemporaries, poorly written, or too revealing of shameful behavior. Out of curiosity I started reading one of my old diaries in the basement and was appalled at the petty immaturity of the person I once was. Some writers I greatly admired, such as Hardy, Dickens, Kafka, and Larkin, had burned their papers rather than let them fall into the hands of malicious, prying biographers. But they possessed nobler characters than I. Fortunately, modesty precluded me from imagining there would be a rush of biographers competing to write my Life anytime soon. Thus I vacillated between worrying that damaging secrets would get out and wondering if anyone would ever decide to work on my archive. Oh well, either way, it was too late; let it all hang out.

When the library worker from Yale arrived in his white panel truck, I opened the top latch on the basement and helped him load the boxes, which he lifted up to me. It took a whole morning. As he drove away, I was hit by a profound ache, immediately missing these proofs of having lived, which had always surrounded me protectively. I felt utterly denuded. Talk about a phantom limb! But I also felt enormous relief, just getting these accumulated exertions out of the house. A burden was lifted from me; I could start all over again to accumulate records of my folly.

Summers in Vermont

FOR THE PAST FIFTEEN YEARS, we—my wife, my daughter, and I—have been renting summer houses in July or August in the same Londonderry/Weston area of southern Vermont. We started out renting for a whole month, but have recently scaled it down to two weeks. In the beginning I thought of these getaways as something I did for my daughter, Lily, whose school chums also summered or went to camp in the area, and for Cheryl, who loves the country and is always fantasizing about someday having a second home in a leafy sheltered nook overlooking a mountain landscape. I am less picky about the need for a vista, and as a city rat devoted to New York, I have long resisted buying a country house, not only because we can't afford it but because I don't fancy being torn between two domiciles, urban and rural. The thought of getting in a car every Friday night and driving several hours north for the questionable serenity of playing weekend country squire, then driving back in traffic jams Sunday night, gives me the willies.

So it came as a surprise to me that I was the one who insisted on renting our usual house in Vermont this year, though my daughter, who had recently graduated from college, would be working at a job in the city in August, and my wife was all for scouring the internet to find a cheaper rental with a better view, more dependable Wi-Fi, and less lumpy couches. I had become attached to our secluded rented house in Weston, at the end of a dirt road, with enough bedrooms to quarter a regiment. Many of these Vermont houses for rent are really designed as ski lodges, winter is their high season: they are characteristically adorned with abominably ugly platters by the local potter, mounted taxidermy, wooden ducks, or plastic bears. One does not expect to encounter the same sophisticated Bauhaus-inspired minimalist interior design aspired to in city digs, but part of the adventure is adjusting to a different aesthetic, homier if homelier. I was almost looking forward to those lumpy orange couches, so low-backed as to force bodily contortions while trying to watch television.

The point is, I did not want to have to *think* about anything: I wanted to go on automatic pilot, knowing where the nearest supermarket and restaurants and swimming holes were, aware that I would have to surrender at some point to the magnetic field of the Vermont Country Store, with its sharp cheddar cheeses and frumpy flannel pajamas. In fifteen years we had more or less explored every small town and hiking trail in the area, so there was no need to undertake any excursions or indeed to discover anything new. I could simply read, eat, play tennis, nap, and empty out—healing, if possible, in time for the demanding teaching year that would begin in September.

That's exactly how it is working out. I discover my pores responding to the verdant woods, gratefully breathing in the familiar Green Mountains landscapes, all of which transpires on an unconscious level. It's unconscious partly because I am so ignorant about nature, and can only take in the trees and the clouds as immanent spirits without being able to identify them by name or spot any changes in their condition from one year to the next. At night,

Cheryl tells me to look up at the stars, so plentiful and visible: I oblige for a few seconds, but do not like craning my neck that far. A friend asked if I have been watching the Perseid meteor shower the last few nights, and I said of course, though I had no idea what he was talking about. I may not understand a thing about the natural world surrounding me in the country, but at least I now know, at long last, that I need it as oxygen: the city is not enough.

Tennis, Anyone?

EVERYONE SHOULD HAVE an activity or hobby they're not very good at. Mine is tennis. It is quite educational, especially for someone like me with a superiority complex, to struggle for decades trying to acquire a skill without being able to rise above mediocrity. I used to tell myself it was because I had started late, in my twenties, having had no tennis courts around me as a boy growing up in ghetto Brooklyn. According to this excuse, what counts are the thousands of balls you hit mindlessly before you go to college, which get converted into "muscle memory." But surely, having played for decades, I should have compensated for that early deprivation by now and acquired that blessed muscle memory. No, what I lack is talent. Also, the sort of physical intelligence athletes have that allows them to dart for the ball as soon as it leaves the racket or bat. Instead I wait for it to land some distance away and then lamely run after it. Often I tell myself that it's too far away, I'll never reach it. Though I'm fairly consistent at returning the ball, and don't usually double-fault on the serve, I play too cautiously. It's rare that I smash winners; I wait for the other players to mis-hit, and when they don't, I accept the defeat as preordained. No tennis teacher has ever been able to recalibrate my fatalism.

I have been taking tennis lessons off and on for most of my adult life. There was the vain teacher, Hal, God's gift to women, who boasted that he used to spend several months each year in Costa Rica giving lessons and bedding his students. He never bothered to tell me I was hitting the ball too flatly. There was Francis, the Sri Lankan, a lovely, pudgy, middle-aged family man who taught me to take the ball "on the rise"; the only problem with him was that his accent was so thick, I could rarely make out what he was saying. My favorite tennis teacher of all time is Todd, with whom I have been taking lessons the last four years. I like him best because he has a good sense of humor, tolerates ineptitude, is gifted at breaking down the mechanics, and treats tennis as an opportunity to have fun, not a matter of life and death. During breaks we discuss politics, usually agreeing, and we tease each other; he pretends to be inarticulate, and I pretend that I am going to rough him up. Often he will compliment me with "Nice shot!" or say "Good work!" at the end of the hour. Sometimes, though, he slips and the truth comes out. Last week I thought I had played rather well, and I asked him, "How do you think I did?" He got a distracted look in his eye, as though he wished I hadn't cornered him, and said, "You were okay. But you need to follow through more, and speed up your swing."

My heart sank. I realized how hopelessly incorrect my form must look to him. I felt sorry for him, suddenly equating his situation with a violin teacher whose student keeps playing off-key or who you know will never improve. From my end, I value his approval immensely. The fact that I see him for an hour once a week makes him one of the most important people in my life. Having pried, I know a fair amount about him: he studied Russian literature in college, decided to play tennis, never got very far on the professional circuit; his parents, academics, divorced; his father is dead, his mother old and frail, and he flies home to the Midwest periodically to visit her; he plays in a rock band on weekends, seems to be separated from his wife, has a son, and is around fifty. Beneath his jesting exterior I sense melancholy, but perhaps I am only projecting from what I know of his background. You would think the study of Chekhov, Gogol, and the other Russians might have prepared him better for life's disappointments, such as having mediocre pupils like me.

He has been trying to get me to hit the ball with more spin, by keeping it on my racket longer and "brushing" it, whatever that means. Sometimes I do it accidentally, and he thinks I am getting the hang of it. He will pantomime what I should do more of, indicating why the shot went wrong. "Use your words," I tell him, like the English professor I am. I must find *some* ways to assert my superiority.

This week I tried harder to concentrate on following through and hitting with pace. I went for angles more. His response was encouraging. In truth, I think my game is sharpening a little, by infinitesimal degrees. It's becoming cagier, if no more powerful than before. By the time I reach ninety, I should be able to summon the nerve to enter the club's senior tournament.

They say the only way to improve your game is to hit with players who are better than you. What the cliché doesn't say is that it can be humiliating for you and excruciatingly frustrating for the other players. Every year, when I vacation in Vermont, I fall in with a bunch of tennis players, retired for the most part, who are all far more agile—they were maybe on their college tennis team and remain remarkably fit—but who let me participate out of basic kindness. This year, at the beginning of the daily fortnight sessions I was terrible. I had regressed, and to see the look of chagrin on my doubles partner's face when I misplayed a ball made me think of giving up the sport forever. By the end of the first week my timing had picked

23

up, or maybe my muscle memory had kicked in, and I was able to hold my own. Toward the end of my two weeks, they were anointing me Most Improved Player. This was not the first time I had been so designated. I get it that you can only be "most improved" if you were lousy to begin with. But I will take that accolade, and hope to build on it in the coming year.

Confronting the Inevitable Subject

I suppose I can no longer avoid writing about the subject that is on everyone's lips: Donald J. Trump. It makes me queasy to write about him, because I don't think I have anything original to say, nothing that hasn't been analyzed and reprinted a million times. In general, I have tried not to worry too much about the political campaign, I have even made myself promise not to panic, nor to let it spoil my summer. And yet I find myself obsessing about this man, who nightmarishly haunts me like a demented Porky Pig. What is it about him that is so transfixing? He says such idiotic things, which no American politician before has ever dared utter: deriding the parents of a dead soldier, or vowing to block Muslims from entering the country, or claiming he can get no justice from an American-born judge with Hispanic roots, or mocking John McCain because he was a POW. We all know the list, and I looked forward each week to hearing some new, outrageously imbecilic pronouncement added to it, even as I cringed at the latest affront.

There is certainly something fascinating about stupidity, especially when it is blatantly made public: it becomes a kind of negative intelligence. Oh, I know, he may be cunning and bright in his way (so they say), but the real attraction, the essence of his charisma, is that he is remarkably stupid. Not crazy, just stupid. And proud of it. Or doesn't know he is stupid. He reads nothing, he only watches television news. He is like a Black Hole of Intellect. I, who have spent my whole life pathetically trying to snatch a few grains of intelligence, cannot help but see him as my polar opposite.

Before the Republican National Convention, I would sometimes watch the man giving speeches, intrigued for ten minutes by his declarative sentences of eight words or less, by the glibness with which he lied, by his egotistical self-flattery and the Mussolini profiles he struck. But then, during the week of the RNC, I couldn't take it anymore: I was horrified, revolted, I had to switch to the Mets game when Trump launched into his sinister acceptance speech. I could no longer find him perversely entertaining; rather, he seemed to be hectoring me personally, reaching through the television set to insult and bully me. He was saying to me: "You, bookworm, I have no use for you and your kind. You're weak! I will trample you."

It frightened me. And beyond that, it made me feel lonely. If this is the standard by which masculine success is judged in our country, then I must accept forever being an outsider. Ever since high school, when I realized that I was somewhat different from most other students—a too-sensitive nerd (though we didn't have that word then), an egghead, we called it—I have made my peace with abnormality. It didn't bother me: normal was never an option. But somehow, Donald J. Trump, by his very self-presentation, has plunged me back into insecurity. I even question my right to speak up, if I cannot counter his challenge to the life of the mind with dazzling, original witticisms.

I suspect all writers identify with immigrants, struggling to fit into or at least accommodate the often alienating mass culture in which they find themselves. So when Trump goes on the attack against potential immigrants, such as my grandparents who came to this country, I feel personally vulnerable, diminished.

The civic-minded side of me thinks this is nonsense. I must do all I can to defeat this charlatan: time to ring doorbells, make cold calls, send Hillary Clinton more money. Aside from her many qualifications for the Oval Office, she is a politician, which is to say, someone who alters her position based on what is achievable at any moment. And so what? Are we such purists, such moralists, that we expect our leaders to be consistent or saintly? But Donald J. Trump is another story. He is *not* a politician, or he would never say the things he does. He is evil, in the specific sense in which Socrates defined the word: evil is a kind of ignorance. I don't understand the type of man who would embrace ignorance with gusto. It's all I can do to squeeze out these few hundred words about Mr. Trump—and from now on, let's expect to hear no more about him in this blog.

The Missing Friend

OVER THE COURSE of the past twenty years, I have lost half a dozen friends to death. In almost every instance, after the initial shock and sorrow, I adjusted to the loss; but about two years ago my friend Peter suddenly passed away, and I cannot seem to get over it. Why this one death seems harder to accept—more so than my parents'—is baffling me. I suppose it's partly that we expect our aged parents to die, but Peter was a few years younger than I. He had always seemed youthful, boyish even.

We had been good friends for more than forty-five years, from 1969 when we first met as coworkers at the 16 mm rental firm Audio Brandon—I at the time in their San Francisco branch, Peter in their New York office. We came together initially because of our shared love of movies. He had a much greater appetite for violent action pictures and blockbusters than I did, and would mock my enthusiasm for the latest art film from Taiwan or Romania, but he caught up with them as well. His taste in the arts was formidably developed, especially when it came to classical music. You could disagree with him on matters of taste, but never hope to prevail.

I was attracted to him partly because he was so handsome, or, rather, striking: tall, thin, with curvy black hair cut short. He dressed beautifully, like an Italian count. Though only half Italian, on his father's side, he embraced the elegance of that national style in cuisine, couture, and, above all, manners. I met Peter's family at the church memorial for him, and they seemed nice, ordinary people, a little stunned that this highly stylized creature had emerged from their midst.

When I first met him he was engaged to a woman named Christine, who bought him a membership in a swimming pool, which he never managed to use. A telling omen, that. The engagement was broken off, I suspected because he had decided that he was gay. Peter kept his romantic life private, however, and would never explicitly declare himself homosexual. His good manners and congeniality were a form of reserve, a protection of his privacy. I am a nosy guy, and unlike the stereotype some women have of male friendship, that we just talk about sports and guy things, I like to probe and share intimacies. Besides, as his good friend of many years, I thought I had a right to ask. He was evasive, to say the least. To the degree I could get him to talk about it, he seemed to regard himself as bisexual; moreover, he seemed to think it tacky to derive one's identity from sexual preference. I was frustrated at times by his indirectness, trying as I did to press every relationship into an increasingly confessional frame.

Once, when I was going through a hard time emotionally, I told him I was thinking of suicide. He looked very uncomfortable, and I realized that he did not want this sort of thing from me; he expected me to exude a reliable put-togetherness. I knew I had other friends whom I could engage about my vulnerability, and I let it drop. One thing Peter taught me was that you can be very close to someone without necessarily discussing at great length your feelings. He was more willing to talk about his latest job and its challenges. What mattered most to him was professionalism. His motto was: Get On with It, Don't Whine.

I too aspire to professionalism, with its inevitable component of stoicism, and I took him as my model. I watched as he ascended from the vice presidency of one nonprofit organization to the next. He was the perfect Number Two man; his specialty was development, or fundraising, and he had the diplomatic savoir faire necessary to massage wealthy donors. He also had rather precise notions of office procedure and working within a chain of command. I would listen with fascination to his discourses on the managerial side of things, which seemed so much more grown-up than the shaggy literary-academic milieu in which I operated. During the Carter administration, his disapproval of Jimmy Carter had less to do with White House policies than with the amateurish gaffes of Carter's staff, mostly clueless Georgia cronies.

Peter had definite ideas about everything: One morning, he was shaving and he solemnly volunteered the opinion that the disposable razor in his hand was "a very good product." I had to laugh, it sounded so much like a TV ad. What he decided to admire never failed to intrigue me. He loved Klondike Bars. He was very well-informed, would go through a stack of reading matter, including *The New York Review of Books*, the *London Review of Books*, *The New Republic*, *The Nation*, *The Wall Street Journal*, and current nonfiction books, in a weekend. He would become obsessed with a topic for weeks on end. Why did he care so much about Roman Polanski, for instance? He kept urging that I write a biography of Polanski. Then there was his anti-Zionist period, which made for an awkward passage in our friendship, since I, though certainly no fan of Netanyahu, felt a little more sympathetic to Israel than he did. Peter, ever the diplomat, got the hint and stopped fulminating on the topic.

He was an extremely generous host, so long as you surrendered to his mise-en-scène. When I visited him in his house upstate in Stuyvesant Falls, New York, he would plan out every detail beforehand: what to eat for breakfast, where to drive in the area, what DVDs to watch at night. If I sometimes bristled at his level of control, it is as much for these eccentricities, quirks, and rigidities that I miss him now.

He was very proud of me, would come to my readings, buy my books, send me notes about them, and offer advice about how to promote myself as a writer. I especially miss him this summer, because we used to visit him in his upstate home in June or July, and in return he would spend a few days with us in our Vermont rental. He was one of those rare friends who showed warmth toward and interest in my wife and daughter as well as myself. I will miss him, too, when the New York Film Festival starts in September: We would regularly confer each year about what tickets to buy and attend screenings together. It was one of our many rituals. He would grouse about the slipshod, "scandalous" way the Film Society of Lincoln Center handled members' orders, for which he seemed to hold me personally responsible. As usual, he was preoccupied with organizational systems and public relations.

He lived alone. Perhaps he felt more in control that way. He would venture forth and see friends, of which he had many, go to concerts and movies with them, and then (I see him in my mind's eye) come back home, kick off his loafers, not have to humor anyone but himself—and his beloved German shepherd, Hannah. I, who had written a book about bachelorhood before settling into family life, envied his solitude a little. His was the road not taken.

The week before he died, I was on the phone with him, volunteering to come up to the hospital where he was being treated for some complications from a previous condition. (I always wondered if he'd had AIDS—I could never be sure one way or the other.) He said he would not want me to see him in his present state, but would be glad for me to visit once he had undergone a particularly risky course of action. I gathered that blast of radiation and chemo would either cure him or kill him. It did the latter. I felt cheated that I had not been allowed to see him one last time.

In trying to puzzle out why he is so present in my mind, why I find it so hard to accept his death with equilibrium, I ask myself, "Could it be that I was in love with him?" Not exactly, any more than I am a little in love with all my friends. I think it has more to do with the ways that we were alike and unalike, and the differences between us that stimulated my imagination. He lived alone, by most appearances serenely so. He was corporate, gay for the most part (though I think his last years may have been largely celibate), Catholic, reserved—and formal. It's that formal quality I cherished and miss most, in the end. Once, I visited him in his office, and his secretary said, in the spirit of sharing a joke about our mutual acquaintance, "The Monsignor will see you now."

The Dead of Summer

IT'S THE DEAD OF SUMMER, and my brain shuts down. *I'm hot*, I think. Then ... *I'm hot! It's so hot. I think I'll lie down on the couch for a bit and read.* A good thing that the couch is large enough to accommodate my prone six-foot body. No sooner do I arrange the pillows and read a few pages than my eyes close. I am taking a nap, a summer nap, which is generally the only kind I do take. I don't know why I can't seem to nap in the fall or winter, though everyone tells me it's good for one's health, no shame in it whatsoever. I agree, but unless a drowsiness brought on by heat overtakes me and literally forces me toward the solace of the couch, I can't do it. A summer nap is delicious, I feel my mouth coated with a milky gummy substance, and I surrender to somnolent passivity, awakening only to the sounds coming through the window. There is nothing I can do for the moment to make the world a better place, to improve my family's condition, or to articulate intriguing, counterintuitive insights that might someday adorn my writing. In fact, I am blissfully inarticulate. For most of the year, being a college professor, I am obliged to provide answers to my students' questions, to think on my feet and play Mr. Encyclopedia. The upside, for those like myself who toil in academia, is summer vacation, when for three and a half months I can be stupid. In the course of daily conversation with my wife and daughter I fail to finish my sentences, trail off, mumble; it

seems not worth the bother to shape my thoughts into crisp forma-
tions. This maddens them, rightly so. They think I am turning into
a slug.

Of course I read a lot in the summer—when I can keep my eyes
open. Charles Lamb once wrote: "I cannot sit and think. Books
think for me." How true. We writers are supposed to be thinking
for ourselves all the time, which would be admirable indeed if it
were possible. Instead, just to get the old brain going, I often thumb
a ride on another's thought currents. If I am on deadline to write a
book review, I sit on the toilet paging though the *London Review
of Books*, *The New York Review of Books*, *The Times Literary Supplement*, *Bookforum*, *The American Scholar*—whatever comes easiest
to hand in the pile of periodicals beside the bathroom sink—just to
remind myself of the worldly, expert tone I am expected to affect.
Then I write a few pages and—take a nap.

What if I have nothing to say? The challenge of keeping a blog
such as this one, in my view, is to write precisely about nothing and
somehow fill up five hundred words with improvised filigree, like a
jazz pianist playing block chords while waiting for the star saxophonist to return to the stage. Flaubert dreamed of writing a book
about nothing, no plot or characters, just the sheer charm of prose
style. I am no Flaubert, so I have to at least pretend to follow a topic.
Let's see, where were we? Summer patterns. I tend to take a shower
daily in the summer, because otherwise I will feel sticky or get heat
rashes, whereas in the winter I can go two or three days in a row
without showering.... But you don't need to know that, it's of no
consequence to anyone except my wife. The frequency of my showering may in fact constitute the outer limit of what is permissible to
write about in a blog.

Okay, then, searching for other summer behaviors, I eat lots of corn and peaches, drink lemonade, and beer becomes essential. When I drink a cold beer in the evening I feel myself expanding with gratitude, like a thirsty plant watered by a garden hose on a timer. I also watch a good deal of baseball, and if my team, the Mets, are having a mediocre year, then my summer turns gloomier. Fortunately, this year they still have a chance.

I would just like to conclude by saying that if this blog had been written during the winter months, the sentences would have been far more crisp and elegant, the analysis deeper, and the vocabulary more surprising.

Remembering Abbas Kiarostami

ON JULY 4, a great artist and a remarkable human being, Abbas Kiarostami, died—unnecessarily, as it turns out. I knew him slightly, having interviewed him several times and written about him often. He was, to my mind, not simply the greatest Iranian filmmaker but one of the two or three greatest filmmakers alive (and now I have to amend that last word). Though his name barely registered to the American public, he was a revered figure in the international film festival circuit. He began making shorts about children, having been invited to start the filmmaking branch of the Institute for the Intellectual Development of Children and Young Adults. From these shorts he graduated to superb feature films, such as *Homework*, *Close-up*, *Where Is the Friend's House?*, *And Life Goes On*, *Through the Olive Trees*, *The Wind Will Carry Us*, and *Taste of Cherry*, which combined neorealist humanism in the tradition of Roberto Rossellini, Vittorio De Sica, and Satyajit Ray with a formalist rigor (choreographed long-duration shots) and a playful, postmodernist self-referentiality. In a sense, he solved the dichotomy between fiction and documentary. His films were gifted with patient observation and curiosity about ordinary people; there were always humorous bits, they breathed naturally, and they were healthy for you—that is, they made you feel engrossed, in suspense yet at peace when watching them.

Here is an excerpt from an interview I did with him, which conveys that thoughtful part of his sensibility:

PL: I have a question about your sense of pace. Your movies have these alternations of tension and relaxation, of stillness and conflict. Some scenes seem to go on a long time, and then at other times the drama is very condensed.

AK: That rhythm is based on nature, life: you know, day, night, summer, winter. The contrast between these things is what sustains our interest, because even if you love spring, you can't have spring all year long or you'd get bored. I think there is a pace to nature, and if you adopt the same pace to your films, in the sense that you manipulate it—at some point caress it, at some point be rough with it—that will cause interest.

PL: I wonder if it's also a cultural difference, because American movies are becoming more and more constant action. You'd rarely get a sequence in an American film like the one in *Through the Olive Trees* where the two old men are philosophizing, since it doesn't "advance the plot," so to speak.

AK: I'm really enjoying this conversation, because these are the kinds of things that I was always thinking about, but no one ever brought them up. So I worry that maybe they don't understand. In the most recent example, *Through the Olive Trees*, we were making a movie about making a movie, but there were moments in the film when we weren't "doing" anything. I was even sometimes tempted to put black leader in between the scenes—because I was constantly hunting for scenes in which there was "nothing happening." That nothingness I wanted to include in my film. Like in *Close-up*, where somebody kicks a can. But I needed that. I needed that "nothing" there.

PL: Do you need it for aesthetic or spiritual reasons? Or both?

AK: At some point those two intersect. If you bring out the aesthetic aspect, then maybe you'll see a reflection of the spiritual as well. The points where nothing happens in a movie, those are the points where something is about to bloom. They are preparations for blooming, similar to a plant which has not emerged from the earth yet, but you know there are roots there and something is happening. . . . So when people tell me "Your movie slows down here a little bit," I love that! Because if it didn't slow down, then I couldn't lift it again.

Through his films and his bearing, Kiarostami embodied the antithesis of the scary fundamentalist image we were being bombarded with in Western media about Iran. He felt no obligation to make art that polemically criticized the mullahs, that was not his style, but you were never in doubt of his cosmopolitan, secular sympathies. He was a very handsome man, and a natty dresser, who carried himself with aristocratic elegance and always wore sunglasses. Before our interview I met Kiarostami and his translator in a hotel lobby near Lincoln Center, and we went upstairs to his room, where the translator immediately drew the blinds, explaining that "sunlight is the enemy of Mr. Kiarostami." So the sunglasses were not an affectation of cool. Before we could begin, my mother-in-law rang my cell phone, warning me to be on the alert: she was nervous about my getting stuck with this Iranian Muslim in a hotel room. I joked about it with Kiarostami. Many years later, as I was interviewing him again, this time about his marvelous Japanese-language picture *Like Someone in Love* at the New York Film Festival, he suddenly cried out in the middle of the event: "I remember now, the last time your mother-in-law cautioned you about me!" The audience had a good laugh.

Women were always buzzing around Kiarostami, trying to snare him. He was undoubtedly courtly, but I am not sure he was a ladies' man. Rather, he gave off a discreet *noli me tangere* signal, underneath the cordial manners. I learned from a documentary about him that he liked nothing better than to go off alone to remote places in nature, where he would take photographs (a medium he came to like more than motion pictures, possibly because he could practice it by himself) and write poems. He knew hundreds of Persian poems by heart and published five volumes of his own poetry. Not the typical film director, in this respect as in so many others. His publisher and best friend said that Kiarostami confided in him that he had felt lonely all his life, though is there really any contradiction between a highly sensitive person's sense of loneliness and his desire to go off and be alone?

I said earlier that he died unnecessarily. The *New York Times* obituary got it wrong, saying the cause of death was cancer. Here is what I learned from Kiarostami's champion, the film programmer Peter Scarlet: "He went into a hospital to have an intestinal polyp checked. The doctor, whom he trusted, left for the Nowruz (New Year's, first day of spring) holiday, and had an assistant handle 'this simple job.' But both overlooked the fact that Abbas, who'd had heart surgery a year earlier, was still taking blood thinners. So after the surgery, they couldn't stop the bleeding. Yes, normally a polyp is checked not with surgery but with a colonoscopy. But for the same thing, they cut Abbas open. Finally, after weeks in the ICU, to the relief of his friends, he was flown to Paris, where it was too late to save him. Now the motherfucking medical people in Iran, who are saying they can't discuss the case because it's a 'medical secret,' are blaming the French doctors!"

So ended the life of the noble filmmaker Kiarostami at age seventy-six. We, sitting where we are, might second-guess his decision to trust the Iranian medical system, but it was characteristic of his attachment to his country. For all that he had started to make more and more of his films abroad, he still identified with Iran's ancient culture and with its contemporary people. He loved trees and, as he once said, you don't uproot a tree.

British Women Novelists

THIS PAST YEAR I have been reading various British women novelists of the second half of the twentieth century: specifically, Muriel Spark, Iris Murdoch, Barbara Pym, and Elizabeth Taylor. I'm not doing it as an assignment or a subject for an essay, I simply fell into the habit of taking one of these novels whenever I was about to fly off somewhere. The books are generally short, about 220 pages, clever, wise, satisfying, and delightfully written—so much so that it has made me wonder why I had been avoiding their authors for so long. It could not simply be sexism, since I have been drawn to female writers at least as much as to males. I think it had something to do with their reputations as minor (though I often love minor writers the most)—or not just minor but cozy and artistically conventional. I see now that their humbler status, in my mind, had something to do not just with sexism but with not being part of the Modernist project—not extending the experimental advances of James Joyce, T. S. Eliot, Ezra Pound, and Virginia Woolf. They wrote unapologetically in a realist/naturalist manner, and their books were formally shapely, fastidiously structured, and elegantly phrased. There is a tendency for theater majors to look down their noses at the well-made play, and I fear I must have been exercising a similarly snobbish prejudice, until now, against the well-made novel. Perhaps it has something to do with age, but I have reached a point in life when I am grateful for a well-made novel, just as I am for a well-made movie or a well-made pie.

These British women novelists all specialized in the comic novel, capturing the vanities and self-delusions of their characters, while tenderly granting them enough space to make colossal mistakes and sometimes recoup their losses. I finally caught up with Spark's iconic *The Prime of Miss Jean Brodie*, as well as her *Memento Mori* and *The Girls of Slender Means*. This last title I liked the best, because it was her most high-spirited and generous (Spark can be nasty). Similarly, with Murdoch, I was most entranced by her first novel, *Under the Net*, with its breezy portrait of the London and Paris film worlds, though I found *A Severed Head*, *The Bell*, and *The Sea, the Sea* also engaging. Murdoch is very good at delineating male conceit and is not entirely unsympathetic in that regard, though her egotistical men do get their comeuppance. I gobbled up Barbara Pym's exquisite *Less Than Angels, Jane and Prudence,* and *A Glass of Blessings*. I have so far only read a couple of novels by Elizabeth Taylor, *In a Summer Season* and *Mrs. Palfrey at the Claremont*, but they contained such brilliantly observed ensemble portraits that I can't wait to sample more.

All these writers are candid about female sexual desire, which they take for granted without the fuss American novelists make. When I think of the American novels produced at the same time, they seem shaggier, more ambitious, more adolescent, and far less stoical. Take Saul Bellow's *Henderson the Rain King* or Philip Roth's *Sabbath's Theater*, both magnificent yowls of appetite and need. The British women writers I have been discussing are more inclined to view human drives with an ironic, reserved smile. Their characters are smaller, as befits the old saw that tragedy ennobles human beings, while comedy diminishes. The British novelist benefits, even at this late date, from a more defined social class structure, which pins down precise details about individual characters and their backgrounds. Those novels, which are set in country houses, have a tight focus, like a Dorothy Sayers murder mystery. But even some of the urban novels, such as *The Girls of Slender Means*, cling to a single boardinghouse setting, or a schoolhouse, as in *The Prime of Miss Jean Brodie*: there is much less of that gusty wanderlust that you get in American novels. Both are valid, both enrich the literary scene, but I was educated for so long in the expansive American model, *Moby-Dick* etc., that I find it reassuring to settle down occasionally in one place. Could it be that I'm finally becoming an Anglophile, after decades of resisting the complacencies of *Masterpiece Theatre*? No, I just think I value sly, reserved humor and trim structure more than I used to.

What Our Politicians Can't Bring Themselves to Say

I WAS WATCHING the presidential debate, and in the midst of my anxiety and dismay began to wonder: What would happen if certain questions could be truthfully answered? I did not expect truth to issue from Donald Trump, who lies as the nightingale sings, but I do hold Hillary Clinton to a higher standard. For instance, when asked about the discrepancy between her private feelings and public statements, and whether this indicated that she was two-faced, it would have been so refreshing to hear her say: "Of course there is a difference between my private and my public selves, as there is for everyone. That does not mean that I am 'two-faced,' in the sense of being a hypocrite. Because I am a complex human being and have an inner life, there are many aspects to my consciousness. Moreover, I may be in the process of changing my mind while weighing the issues. As Montaigne says, man is inherently variable and inconsistent, and moreover, we must keep a private storehouse just for ourselves—"

Okay, maybe it wouldn't be such a good idea for her to quote Montaigne. As it is, instead of owning up to her own complexity she took the indirect route of citing Abraham Lincoln, as the precedent of a great leader strategizing in order to push through a controversial policy. All true, and a fairly intellectual answer at that, but Trump pounced on her and said she was trying to hide her false self behind honest Lincoln. Strange, this political game of "gotcha" and accusing one's opponent of flip-flopping, which fails to take into account the truth of Walt Whitman's assertion, "Do I contract myself?/Very well then I contradict myself, / (I am large, I contain multitudes.)" (Hmm. Maybe it's just as well she left Whitman out of it.)

Another example: Both candidates asserted that they had a plan to wipe out ISIS. They must know—certainly Hillary does, being an experienced diplomat—that there is little chance for all manifestations of jihadism to disappear in our lifetime. Even if you were to eradicate ISIS, it would doubtless spring up in another form, given the persistence of anti-Western resentment, power-vacuum-fueled nationalism, and competition for resources. Moreover, we can continue to expect lone-wolf psychopaths who will latch on to any cause as the impetus to shoot up malls and nightclubs.

Regarding a candidate like Hillary's "contamination" by Big Money: We're living in a capitalist society, and it is virtually impossible for any national politician not to interact with, or accept the support of, wealthy players. That does not necessarily mean that one is a puppet of the oligarchy, or that one cannot still press effectively when in office for a progressive agenda.

Also, while it's entirely understandable and even appropriate for presidential candidates to express a patriotic love for their country, why must it take the exaggerated form of asserting America as the greatest country, the hope of the world, when such self-flattering, exceptionalist boasts of our strength to crush anyone who gets in our way have landed us in such trouble? A little humility and historical perspective would go a long way toward treating the public like adults.

45

Finally, if Donald Trump parades Bill Clinton's ex-lovers in a press conference, why can't Mrs. Clinton simply say: "My husband isn't running for president this year, I am." Perhaps the reason she can't do this takes us back to the original conundrum: her inability to admit that she has both a private and a public self. Hillary is very uncomfortable revealing her interiority. She will talk till the cows come home about policy or recite her résumé, but she shies away from self-reflectiveness. Commentators say she must show more of her "vulnerable" side. I think she is plenty vulnerable, you can watch her face register mercurial emotional shifts, from pleasure to panic to irony to uncertainty to disdain. What she does not do well is articulate her self-awareness and take the voters into her confidence. Some politicians can do that, though it's a gamble and can cause trouble. Remember Jimmy Carter telling *Playboy* he lusted in his heart? Donald Trump is always talking about himself, even in the third person, though it is all braggadocio with nary an insight. I am sure Hillary Clinton has done extensive psychological homework on herself, in private, but she is too guarded to show it to us. That is why some find her too "coached." To loosen up her capacity for revealing her inner self, I recommend she take a personal essay–writing class. I would be more than happy to teach it, though some of my colleagues in Washington, D.C., might do it as well, if they can pry her away from her presidential duties.

September Song

My favorite time of the year is September. Despite the groans of everyone, including myself, regarding the end of summer, the truth is that by Labor Day I am more than happy to get back to work and a regular routine. If summer carries with it the promise of transformation, of exploring other potential selves one might hope to stir awake through travel and leisure, it can also place one in frightening contact with one's emptiness and shallowness. My embrace of September is therefore founded on the relief that I can return to my essentially limited but dependable self-repertoire.

There is also something about the light at this time of year—a crisper sun kissing the leaves of trees, an extra blueness in the sky. I've always been intrigued by those mini-essays about the changing of seasons by some nature writer like Verlyn Klinkenborg, which would appear at the foot of the *Times* editorial page. I wish I could summon that knowingness about flora and fauna as it relates to the seasons and indulge in a few paragraphs of lyrical twaddle. No chance of that happening; and in any case, my whole appreciation of this time of year is governed by a quickening pulse in the urban calendar: the arrival of big exhibits in the museums, the start of the New York Film Festival with its challenging parade of world cinema (after a sleepy summer of comic-book-derived sequels and animated family pictures), the excitement of the baseball season's final month (especially if one's team is vying for a wild card), the U.S. Open tennis tournament, the Jewish High Holidays (the one time of year I can be counted on to go to synagogue), and of course, for those of us on an academic schedule, the return to school.

For me, each New Year begins not on January 1st but on the first day of classes. I must then emerge from my interior retreat, my laconic vegetative stupor, and perform that public act of eloquent assertion and flimflam showmanship known as teaching. It can be a wrenching transition, I am not alone in feeling frightened before the first day: Colleagues I have spoken to, who've been at it even longer than I have, report butterflies in the stomach, a tightening chest, and the equivalent of stage fright. Fortunately, that first day I can get away with passing out syllabi and dismissing the class early. It is in the second week that I truly have to pull myself together.

This September was the first one in memory that I was no longer in sync with my daughter's schedule. Lily, having graduated from college in May, secured a job shortly after and is taking the subway into downtown Manhattan every morning, while I alone return to the groves of academe. I feel like a dumb overgrown boy in high school who has been left back. As I get older and older, the students, the new crop, remain more or less the same age, bursting with youthful promise. There is something wrong with this picture. Ah, let me not think about it! Let me rejoice instead in September's beautiful temperate weather.

Elevated

YESTERDAY I HAD my first MRI. I had scheduled it after a visit to my urologist, Dr. Purohit, whom I had been seeing once a year to check on the status of my prostate. This time he told me that my PSA numbers (one of the means by which your propensity for prostate cancer is checked) were elevated: they had been drifting upwards over the last few visits and were now at 6.3. Dr. Purohit is Indian, in his forties, I imagine, and very handsome, with Kewpie-doll lips. Though I am not gay, I still register and appreciate masculine beauty. His manner is sympathetic, but he once alarmed me by saying that my cancer was not a problem yet, it was under control. I didn't even know I had a cancer. I once read an article which said that over time everyone develops cancer. In any case, the doctor said it would be a good idea to get an MRI, just to be on the safe side. If any lesions or irregularities turned up, then they would do a biopsy.

I went home and told my wife, who reminded me in a calm voice that prostate cancers developed so slowly that often the person would die first before the cancer could kill them. I didn't find this so reassuring, a) because some men do die of prostate cancer, and b) because I wasn't eager to hurry up and die so that I could beat prostate cancer to the punch. She must have realized I thought her attitude a little too blasé, and quickly admitted the situation was "concerning." That was the word, "concerning," that we hit upon as a compromise between my anxiety and her sanguine detachment.

It was rainy, soggy, and blustery yesterday; I got out of the subway and started to walk all the way east to the imaging center. Why do they always put these medical facilities all the way east by the river? On the way I stopped at a food vendor and bought a hot dog, or rather an Italian sausage, because I hadn't had any breakfast and was afraid I would suddenly get too hungry in the middle of the procedure. But I cursed myself for ordering something that needed to be fried, which meant getting soaking wet as I stood in the rain waiting for my food. Even though I had an umbrella, my wide-wale corduroy pants were already drenched, a particularly unpleasant sensation, wet corduroy. I ate the sausage (not bad) as I walked the last few blocks to the center. In the lobby was a plastic-bag dispenser for umbrellas, and I availed myself of one. A curious amenity: What would they think of next? The receptionist gave me a dozen forms to fill out: she was young and pleasant and I saw on her name tag that she had a Greek name. I sat in the waiting room with other patients, who looked disgruntled or out of sorts, and tried to finish the Friday *New York Times* crossword puzzle, which was proving difficult, especially the upper right-hand corner. It was a bad omen when I couldn't finish the day's crossword puzzle. Usually I could somehow solve Friday's and Saturday's puzzles, which are the hardest, but not today's. Maybe my brain was going bad, as well as my prostate.

I noted politely, I hope, at the desk, that my appointment was for 11:30 and it was already noon. She apologized, said they were running late. "Five more minutes," I was promised. Sure enough, a young Asian man summoned me not long after and led me through a set of doors to a waiting room, where I was given a hospital gown that opened at the back and told to undress, everything except for my underwear. He advised me to use the bathroom first. I was given a key, and locked the door of the changing room so that my wallet would not be stolen. I did use the bathroom, obediently. Now it was time for my MRI. What do those initials stand for? I never thought to ask. Another young man, who introduced himself as Claudio, shook my hand and told me to lie on the table. "I'm going to take some of your blood," he said, like an affable vampire. "This is going to sting," he warned, and it did. Then he flushed some saline solution into my vein and followed it up with dye.

"How long will the procedure last?" I asked.

"Forty-five minutes. What kind of music do you like?" he asked, putting earphones over my head.

It seemed a tricky question, I like many kinds of music. "Classical," I answered finally. He was about to roll me into the cylindrical machine that looks like some sort of spacecraft. Through the earphones I was hearing a Norah Jones song. I don't hate Norah Jones exactly, but I would not want to enter eternity locked in her lite-pop embrace. "This isn't classical!" I cried out.

"Yes, I was about to change it," he answered, sounding annoyed. "Remember, don't move. Stay very still." He placed a little rubber ball in my left hand and told me that if I needed to call for assistance I could squeeze it. Then he went out of sight.

I was alone—alone in space. Actually it wasn't that dark, not like a sensory deprivation experiment, I could easily make out the cone form encircling me, with its ridged divisions, but I chose to shut my eyes. A series of banging noises started, like an ak-ak gun, and the machine began to wobble and vibrate like an automatic dryer. The noises kept changing in pitch and rhythm. I wondered what would happen if I had a panic attack. Maybe that was why they had given me the little ball, to signal to the outside world. True, I had never had a panic attack, but there was always a first time.... Meanwhile, my earphone music was segueing from some sort of lullaby to Vivaldi's *Four Seasons*. My throat felt dry. I was becoming acutely aware of pins and needles in both my hands, especially the one holding the little ball. A voice from a loudspeaker announced: "This next phase will last seven minutes." Lots of racket and shaking. The plate underneath my buttocks became quite hot. I had not the slightest doubt that I could stoically endure the whole forty-five minutes, though time was moving slowly, inordinately so. "The next, final phase will last ten minutes," the disembodied voice informed me. Oh, good. I could do ten more minutes. The music had evolved to a fully orchestrated Chopin nocturne. Then it was over. Claudio unhooked me. I hadn't minded the experience, it would have been fine except for the pins and needles.

"You should drink several glasses of water during the day, to flush out the dye."

"Otherwise, am I going to glow in the dark?" I jested.

"No, there's no radiation involved with this," he said somberly and proudly. Apparently I'd entered a no-joking zone, like the TSA-operated airport screening lines.

I forgot to drink those several glasses of water.

Holding On to the Banister

IN THE MORNING when I first wake up and go downstairs to feed the cats and get the newspaper from the stoop, I hold on to the banister. I take the steps one at a time, with both feet on each step, because my knees are stiff when I first wake up and I feel a slight pain if I try to take two steps at a time. I often notice while I am still in bed in the morning that I am prone to pulling a muscle, getting a cramp or (my preferred term) a charley horse—which never happened to me when I was young, not that I remember. Sometimes I feel my leg muscle start to cramp up and I halt it just in time by changing positions. All this makes me rather cautious when I first descend the stairs. Sometimes I catch myself thinking about Primo Levi and his fatal tumble: was it suicide or an accident? The scholars are still debating that. In any case, I hold on tightly to the banister in case my foot should slide.

None of this is new: I have always been physically cautious. I remember when I was fourteen and spending the summer as a camp counselor, I walked very slowly and tentatively around the edge of the swimming pool, lest I fall in, little realizing that the head of the camp, Gloria T., was watching me from her cabin window. She, an attractive if authoritarian Black radical community organizer with a sadistic streak, would expose my timidity to all the other counselors in the next group meeting, as proof, I suppose, that I was a softie, lacking in courage. I fought her Stalinist ways every chance I could, but this time I was silenced, as it seemed strange even to me that I had been so timorous in circumnavigating that pool. I'd like to think I was enmeshed in a reverie, that that was why I was proceeding so leisurely, or that I was testing myself to see just how slowly I could traverse the pool's rectangular rim. But probably I was just frightened of falling in.

When my daughter, Lily, was young, we childproofed the whole house, as parents do, putting little metal gates across the top of each flight of stairs. But in time we realized that they were unnecessary, because she invariably held on to the banister, as we had instructed her. She too is physically cautious: she had inherited my DNA and would avoid soccer skirmishes in gym class, instead cheering the others on from the side. How I sympathized with her, while wishing she could have taken after her intrepid mom, who is far more at home in the challenge of objects and nature.

I remember the few times I played football as a child, ending up at the bottom of a scrimmage, and wondering if the pile of bodies would ever get off me before I suffocated. I was not bullied as a child, but neither was I so popular that I could count automatically on the pity of my classmates while gasping for breath. I was also frightened of dogs, after one had pounced on me. I would cross the street, well into adolescence, each time I saw a dog. The entire physical world seemed a minefield, and so it has remained. My clumsiness has always been an effort to forestall some sudden spill. Hence, as I get older I will continue to hold on to banisters (my wife being my principal banister), just to be on the safe side.

On the Death of Friendship

THERE ARE FEW THINGS as mystifying and unnerving to me as the demise of a friendship. I find myself brooding about the few friendships of mine that have cooled, and wondering what went wrong. Was there something I did to offend—some incident I can no longer remember? That would be the best case: usually they dwindled away without specific provocation.

We assume that love affairs are transitory, dependent as they are on the novelty of erotic excitement that habituates in time; but since friendship cooks on a milder, steadier flame, it would seem that, barring some unexpected quarrel, one should be able to stay friends for life. The mistake here is in underestimating the romantic side of friendship, which can exceed that aspect in love affairs: without the benefit of carnal release, there is no ceiling to idealization of the other or projections of spiritual attachment. The friend can seem like your psychic twin, the one you can tell everything to. This mirroring fantasy, essentially narcissistic, may shatter upon the discovery that the other person is indeed a separate individual, with certain peeves that include you, or monomanias that annoy you, or periods of monastic withdrawal into self-absorption, or simply ambitions to travel in a higher social circle than the one you inhabit.

I have lost a few younger friends, who initially looked up to me, by their promotion in the world, which gave them a vaunted sense of self-importance. Now that they were suddenly surrounded by younger persons than themselves who looked up to them for guidance and help in career advancement, they could no longer abide the original terms of the friendship, in which I seemed to hold the upper hand. Perhaps, in responding earlier to their grumbles about not being accorded the worldly respect they felt they deserved, I had counseled patience in what they took to be a condescending manner. Now that they were getting that respect, they may have found my persistent claims of superior wisdom intolerable. I don't know, I can't be sure, because they never avowed any resentment against me. During the cooling-off period, if I tried to confront the matter, they would deny that there was any problem in the friendship. Their resistance took the form of no longer initiating contact, so that I would have to be the one to make the phone calls or send emails; and their vague promises of settling on a date rarely came to pass. If we eventually did get together, for a meal or coffee, they made it seem as though it were purely my imagination that the friendship had died out.

I have also lost friends for the opposite reason: they'd come to regard themselves as failures, and erroneously assumed that I had ascended to a higher plain of accomplishment or celebrity that made me no longer interested in them. I say "erroneously," though there is a grain of truth in their fear that I would find their bitterness and self-pity tiresome. I like to think I am a loyal friend, regardless of the straitened fortunes that may afflict someone I've known for years, but there is a difference between present toleration and prior admiration, which may be too painful to endure on the receiving end.

It's entirely possible that my ex-friends would reject these speculations about power realignments and one-upmanship as completely beside the point. They might say they simply got very busy. Hard as it is for me to fathom such a possibility, maybe they just got bored with me. Shocking as it is to consider that we—who had once been each other's delight—had learned our mutual repertoires and had sucked all the nourishment out of the friendship that was to be had, leaving only a dry husk, one must face up to that possibility. Objectively speaking, I can appreciate that nothing lasts forever, cherry blossoms fall off the trees, as the Japanese are quick to note, and so the waning of friendship should be no more a mystery than mortality itself. Yet I continue to brood about the ones that got away.

As the good doctor, Samuel Johnson, wrote in "Uncertainty of Friendship":

> The most fatal disease of friendship is gradual decay, or dislike hourly increased by causes too slender for complaint, and too numerous for removal. Those who are angry may be reconciled; those who have been injured may receive a recompense: but when the desire of pleasing and willingness to be pleased is silently diminished, the renovation of friendship is hopeless; as, when the vital powers sink into languor, there is no longer any use of the physician.

They say that the older you get, the harder it is to make new friends. There is less space in your life, and perhaps less need. The one exception to the rule, in my case, is that I've been fortunate enough to keep making friends with women. Though most of these women had flourishing literary careers when we first met, with them I found there was less competition, less sibling rivalry; in general, my women friends seem to be more gifted with a capacity for sympathizing with me. Women make better friends. I realize this may sound like one of those empty compliments paid by so-called enlightened males to the female sex, but I am simply recording my experience here. My women friends nurture me incalculably. They are warmer, kinder, better at listening, and know how to flirt gracefully within the confines of a platonic relationship. For whatever reason, the friendships I've had with women have not suffered the same crash-and-burn scenarios that have occasionally marred mine with men. Although, come to think of it, I did lose one close friendship with a woman when I got married. I sensed her irritation that she had lost me as an available plus-one. The women friends I have made since seem more than happy with my marital status; when we get together we can converse pleasurably, wittily, and candidly, without any of that nonsense that comes from having sexual designs on the other. If I still fantasize about enjoying them in bed, that is nobody's business but mine.

On Popularity

THERE IS NO SUBJECT I have been more nervous writing about than being popular and well liked. Contemplating an essay on this topic, I have always drawn back lest I alienate my readers. I would like to be able to explore, as Montaigne did, all the facets of my character and experience, but the royal road of the personal essay is through self-disparagement. There is nothing wrong per se in writing about oneself, observed the nineteenth-century Scottish writer Alexander Smith: "If he be without taint of boastfulness, of self-sufficiency, of hungry vanity, the world will not press the charge home. If a man discourses continually of his wines, his plate, his titled acquaintances, the number and quality of his horses, his men-servants and maid-servants, he must discourse very skillfully indeed if he escapes being called a coxcomb." I have no intention of speaking about my titled acquaintances, horses, or servants, having none, but I do have a lot of friends and well-wishers.

How did that come to be? It should be possible to analyze the situation dispassionately, without vanity. Of course, there is always the possibility that I am deluding myself and am much less popular than I think. I would not be surprised to learn there are plenty of people who detest me or find me irritating, but fortunately I rarely hear from them. In any event, I must face up to the fact that I am regularly being petitioned by friends, acquaintances, ex-students, colleagues, even strangers, to engage with them. Some want advice, others just to bask in my benign glow.

If I think back to when this spate of popularity started, I have to return to elementary school. I took note of several boys who were scapegoats, set upon unfairly by our classmates. They were invariably of the brighter sort, as was I, but there was something strange or foreign in their manner and voice that drew mocking scorn, as to a pretentious affect. I made it a point to appear normal enough, a regular guy, up on the latest fads and popular culture.

When I went on to junior high school, a teacher observed that I had a "hail-fellow-well-met" attitude. I had no idea what that archaic expression meant, but I sensed a criticism: that I had a hearty, genial manner towards everyone, though it was superficial and dismissive underneath. That period of early adolescence can be brutal, with popularity taking on a disproportionate importance. Many of the finest, most sensitive souls fret about their lack of popularity, while the popular ones often seem disingenuous, performative, given to cheap vulgarity. I don't doubt it was a survival strategy for me, rooted in fear.

Regardless, in junior high school I ran for office and was elected the school president; in high school, I was made chief justice of the student court and editor of the literary magazine. This trend of being chosen to lead continued in college, when I became president of a jazz club and a filmmakers' club, and the editor of *The Columbia Review*. Even beyond college, I continued to be chosen to direct various organizations. The question I ask now is: Why were the others so willing to follow my lead? One answer is that they were lazy and happy to let me do the grunt work. But I suspect it also had to do with a display of self-confidence on my part, combined with a chameleonlike ability to meet people on their own terms with a measure of agreeableness.

Where did this self-confidence come from? It seemed to derive from my mother's love for me (for a while I was her favorite child), and with that, an accrual of faith in my abilities whenever and wherever they manifested: a high mark on a test, a well-received speech in front of the assembly, a solo in the choir. Some of it undoubtedly had to do with my being male: I have witnessed too many young women who have demonstrable gifts, but remain beset by insecurity and self-doubt.

As for being agreeable, I have an aversion to angry confrontations, unless pushed to the limit. It was never important for me to be seen as a rebel, and once I had been elevated to a leadership position, I was perfectly willing to engage with the higher-ups—bosses, deans, administrators—as fellow human beings. I like getting my hands dirty with compromise: it suits my love of impurity.

So much for leadership. How and why did I acquire so many friends in my private life? For starters, I made myself available, but not too available. If someone would contact me with a request to get together, I would always reply immediately, suggesting dates. I also recognize part of the duties of friendship is to initiate contact rather than waiting passively for the friend to seek you out. I hate when would-be friends always expect me to make the first move. On the other hand, since my time is limited, those acquaintances on the outer ring of intimacy cannot expect to hear from me that often and must expect to make the first move.

"Do not appear too needy" is a universally recognized law of attraction. When you seem fine by yourself, when you can take it or leave it, people are drawn to you. Though Alexander Smith advises against "self-sufficiency," I have found it to be a very useful posture, actually comforting to others. It takes discipline not to inflict one's sorrows or disappointments on other people in the first ten minutes. I try to be cheerful or at least equable, to smile and let my eyes light up with pleasure on greeting friends. If there is an opportunity for humor or playfulness, I seize it. That means listening to others with both sympathy and detachment, able to convert their troubles into a more general perspective. Listening may be the most important key to popularity. I genuinely prefer getting away from my inner monologue and hearing what others have to say, even if I recognize there should be times when I must be the one to offer confessions, sharing vulnerability.

And I like people, for the most part. When I say I like people, I don't mean I find "the people" necessarily admirable or noble, like some Mexican muralist: I mean that I am moved by an individual's quirks, contradictions, neuroses, as well as his or her brave attempts to circumvent those rigidities. Some individuals I find myself drawn to immediately because of their charm, physical attractiveness, culture, sense of humor, self-awareness. With others, the more solemn types, I see that I am in for a slog, but I regard them with curiosity. The would-be novelist in me pretends I am Balzac, assembling a taxonomy of the human condition.

I am generally well liked by my students. In part it has to do with my work ethic, I try to accommodate their demands. But I also feel a tender sympathy for them, recognizing as I do the patterns behind their problems. They want to become accomplished writers, and I know what that struggle is like, I feel for them. When they describe their roadblocks, my initial response is not "Oh, that's terrible" but

"Yes, that sounds familiar." I can attach it to something I have observed in myself or others.

It helps, in terms of popularity, if you are accomplished in your field and have at least a modicum of power to disperse: others on the lower rungs will seek you out, with requests for blurbs or letters of recommendation. If you can meet these hungry requests with kindness instead of self-protective hauteur, you will not only be sought, you will be well loved. When I was first starting out, as yet unaccomplished and quite powerless, I had to rely on seductiveness to draw people to me. Today, I can assume that my inbox will be filled with fans' flatteries and junior colleagues' attempts to cultivate favor. I do not fool myself that these overtures are necessarily a proof of being well-liked, but they help to swell the sense that I am in demand.

When I asked a dear friend recently to account for my popularity, she said it was because I was "warm and welcoming." My wife scoffed at this explanation, saying that many of my neighbors found me "scary" and remote. She thought I walked around in my head, unaware of others on the block. In her opinion, I was only warm to those who had some intellectual spark that might stimulate me: with the vast portion of humanity, addicted to reality shows and so on, I am bored and show it all too clearly. This may be true. I also know that within the confines of my own house, my wife and daughter find my level of receptivity much more problematic. I suspect I have always been better at friendship than domestic relations. With friends I can be attentive to their needs for limited periods of time, usually less than three hours at a stretch. A good conversation is enough to satisfy them. Loved ones, family members, want more:

they want solutions to their suffering, and I can only fall back on a belief that each of us is alone and must find the strength within to cope with life's injuries.

From the age of thirty on, most of my friends have been in creative fields—writers, filmmakers, visual artists—and have already achieved a measure of success, so that we not only share the peculiar, insular experience of art-making but respect and appreciate each other's efforts. I try to offer them my equanimity as a balm, like a cooling offering in the face of their self-doubts. It's true that the line between asserting equanimity and superiority can be thin, and I have come to dislike my compulsion to feel I have the upper hand, without in any way being able to curb it. But my friends seem to forgive me this flaw as an excusable weakness. I can only assume they find other aspects of my character that compensate for such tiresome shows of conceit.

At times, I've had to be the one to work diplomatically around a writer friend's inflated ego and cosmically expanding self-importance. I've known some difficult, prickly characters who took easy offense. If I've held on to these friendships, it is usually by letting some time pass before reengaging. Not that I am incapable of still losing a friendship, but it happens rarely. When I was younger, in my twenties, I forfeited a number of friends, either through my clumsiness or their wariness.

My turning point came when I relinquished the dream of the one and only best friend, someone with whom you could exchange every thought in a sort of mind meld. Instead I would seek out a variety of friends, each fulfilling a separate destiny, each bringing something different and valuable to me, within their own behavioral boundaries, none expected to ease all my loneliness. Did this alter-

ation, from a romantic search for the psychic match to a promiscuous acquisition of companions, amount to a cynical devaluation of
friendship or a realistic appraisal of human beings' limited capacities,
including my own? I only know that as I grew older, I no longer felt
the same need for a best friend. I could play the field, as those who
would be popular must sign on to do.

The Roads Not Taken

In Jorge Luis Borges's "Borges and I," the Argentine writer draws a distinction between his ordinary self and his writer persona: "The other one, the one called Borges, is the one things happen to. I walk through the streets of Buenos Aires and stop for a moment, perhaps mechanically now, to look at the arch of an entrance hall and the grillwork on the gate; I know of Borges from the mail and see his name on a list of professors or in a biographical dictionary." Similarly, Susan Sontag wrote in her diaries how tired she was of her ostentatious public self, this shrill "Susan Sontag," who had little to do with her quiet, insecure inner core. I do not have this problem: the writer in me has merged with the private self to such an extent that I can no longer see any difference between the two. But I continue to be haunted by the various people I might have been, had I taken a different vocational course when it was offered me.

In junior high school I sang in a Hebrew choir and was told I could become a cantor if I played my cards right. One incentive offered me was that, if I went into the army, I would not have to fight but could stay behind the lines performing liturgical duties. That did not strike me as sufficient reason to become a cantor, particularly as by the time I reached high school I had lost my faith (if indeed I ever had any). So I entered college a prelaw candidate, assuming that, since I was argumentative, I could make a living as an attorney, while writing on the side. However, the siren song of literature pulled me away from the courtroom, and I decided to take my chances scribbling.

I was movie-mad as a young man, and fantasized becoming a film-maker. Unfortunately, I hadn't a penny. The one short film I was able to make, thanks to funds provided by the cameraman's father, taught me that there is a vast difference between a critical appreciation of film and the ability to render convincingly three-dimensional scenes in two dimensions on-screen. If I'd had the good sense to be born into the upper middle class, I might have persisted in filmmaking, but as it was, paper, pen, and typewriter proved to be more within my means.

In one of the several times I underwent psychotherapy, I was told by my analyst that I would make a good therapist. He offered to help me apply to a program. The trouble was, I could not envision sitting on my rump eight hours a day listening to other people's problems. If I could have concocted a peripatetic approach to ther-apy, I might have taken that route. As it was, I had already ruled out the medical profession because I couldn't stand the sight of blood—evidenced by my fainting each time blood was drawn. (I was later told by a physician that that response was fairly common among premed students. In time, he said, I would have circumvented the problem.)

At a loss as to what I might do to earn a living, I took a vocational apperception test. According to the results, I would make a good manager. I was insulted. No thanks, I told myself: I am a poet, an artiste. Years later, when I was teaching at the University of Houston, several of the senior faculty went on leave, and it fell to me to serve as acting director of the creative writing program. I did a decent job during the semester, calling upon what I now saw were my managerial skills: the capacity to make swift decisions and the humane treatment of students and staff (which usually meant bending the punitive rules instead of worrying that it might start a bad precedent). At the end of my term of service I was offered the permanent job of program director, with the suggestion that it might well lead to ascending the ladder of university administration: someday I could become a dean, even a provost! That I had a small talent for managing did not mean I needed to become an academic administrator, and I turned down the offer.

Over the years, I have been asked to apply for jobs as a federal arts education czar, a museum curator, and the editor of a film magazine. I thought hard about each one before declining. Now I wonder about these doppelgängers, these clones who might be running around town: Lopate the cantor, Lopate the lawyer, Lopate the corporate manager, Lopate the psychotherapist, Lopate the editor. Are they the impostors, or am I? I feel their hot breath on my neck as I sit in conference with a student, listening to her problems, or as I direct the nonfiction program at Columbia, or sing lustily along with the cantor during the High Holidays, or edit a friend's manuscript, or make out my will. While I have found minor ways to integrate shards of these various selves I might have been, it does not keep me from pondering the roads not taken. If there is such a thing as reincarnation, it might give me a chance to be reborn as one of these incipient selves. But, given my sins in this lifetime, I will probably return as a rat.

Give Me a Place

In 1563 Michel de Montaigne wrote a long letter recounting the death of his best friend, Étienne de La Boétie. After describing La Boétie's nobly stoical behavior, the very exemplar of a "good death," which he had witnessed at his friend's bedside, Montaigne noted this strange turn toward the end:

> After [his wife] had gone, he said to me: "My brother, stay close to me, please." And then, feeling either the pangs of death sharper and more pressing, or the force of some hot medicine that they had made him swallow, he spoke in a loud and stronger voice, and tossed in his bed with the greatest violence; so that all the company began to have some hope, for until then it was weakness alone that had made us fear to lose him. Then, among other things, he began to entreat me again and again with genuine affection to give him a place; so that I was afraid that his judgment was shaken. Even when I had remonstrated with him very gently that he was letting the illness carry him away and that these were not the words of a man in his sound mind, he did not give in at first and repeated more strongly: "My brother, my brother, do *you* refuse me a place?" This until he forced me to convince him by reason and tell him that since he was breathing and speaking and had a body, consequently he had his

place. "True, true," he answered me then, "I have one, but it is not the one I need; and then when all is said, I have no being left." "God will give you a better one very soon," said I. "Would that I were there already," he replied. "For three days now I have been straining to leave." Shortly after, he breathed his last.

What are we to make of this dying plea to give him a place? More important, what did Montaigne make of it? Some commentators, like Alexander Nehamas in his book *On Friendship*, have argued that the collection of essays Montaigne began writing a decade later, which ensured his lasting fame, became the very "place" he hit upon to honor that request:

> The *Essays* represent the kind of communication Montaigne might have had with La Boétie, regaling him with the sort of stories, incidents, and thoughts that one would share with one's close friends— stories, feelings, and thoughts that range from the most trivial and mundane to the most serious and profound and that, in the process, express their author's personality. But La Boétie was dead; each of the *Essays'* readers assumes his role as the friend to whom Montaigne reveals himself. And in order to communicate the central place that La Boétie held in his life, Montaigne located his essay on friendship, whose hero is La Boétie, in the center of the first volume of the essays. Since what was to become the first volume was all he was planning to write at the time, the essay would have been the centerpiece of the whole book, and the *Essays* would have revolved around it. In addition, Montaigne also included in the essay the text of La Boétie's political treatise, *On Voluntary Servitude*.

However, Montaigne subsequently decided to scrap his friend's thesis, fearing that it was too controversial, and, as we know, went on to write two more volumes of essays, thus relegating La Boétie to a much more peripheral place in the greater scheme.

I thought about La Boétie's urgent entreaty the other day when I was sitting in the synagogue during Rosh Hashanah services. Several of the prayers contained the insistent plea to "inscribe us in the Book of Life." Since Rosh Hashanah is the Jewish New Year, it made sense that one would ask the Deity permission to re-up for another twelve months. One was, in effect, asking like La Boétie for a place in a book. It came to me with a mild flush of shame that in my own life I had replaced the Torah with Montaigne's *Essays* as the defining inspirational text.

My daughter used to ask me, "Why do you even go to synagogue when you don't believe in God?" True enough, I did not, probably from the time I was thirteen, but I hoped that there might still be room, or a place, in my birth religion for atheists, skeptics, and agnostics such as myself. I went in order to hear the songs and to revive nostalgic memories of my youth in a Hebrew choir. More recently, my daughter asked me, "We're *culturally* Jewish, right, Daddy?" Her question pained me, since I would like to believe that there is more to my attachment to Judaism than matzo ball soup, Jackie Mason jokes, and *Fiddler on the Roof* revivals. What does that "more" consist of, exactly? I ask myself. Is it even theological in nature? All I could come up with was a warm feeling toward Judaism's bookish, exegetical tradition, and its emphasis on generosity and social justice. I assiduously swerved away from contemplating Israel's harsh treatment of the Palestinians, saving that awkward subject for another day. In the meantime, I was lulled into peace and repose by listening to the service in Hebrew, a language I don't understand, which provided an opportunity for me to remain in a dreamlike reverie. Indeed, as I sat there I started writing this blog in my head.

Wasn't Montaigne himself part Jewish on his mother's side? If so, that might go a small way toward resolving the guilt of my defection.

The Workmen

I AM NOT HANDY. Though I can make a living by my pen, and write or bullshit about almost any subject under the sun short of economics and physics, I am completely incompetent in the use of other tools. When something breaks down, I don't even try to fix it; my first instinct is to call in the plumber, the roofer, the garage mechanic. These people are professionals, they know what they're doing. Or should. But in fact I don't even make the call, I simply turn the problem over to my wife, who is not only very good at fixing things on her own but has an eagle eye for correct workmanship and can easily spot a shoddy shortcut, patchy paint job, or unserviceable tool. Her first husband was an artist who moonlighted as a carpenter, and she may have picked up from him considerable amounts along these lines. He died while still in his forties; after several years of widowhood she remarried this wordsmith, me, and has more or less resigned herself to my tinkering limitations, though I can't help suspecting her notions of proper masculinity include being handy, which I am not.

A house is an unending project, and over the years we have employed a series of workmen to try to bring our brownstone to a more finished state, or simply to repair cracks, leaks, and other unforeseen emergencies. Typically, my wife will get a referral from a friend or neighbor about some jack-of-all-trades who is really good at odd jobs—and cheap. Since we are on a tight budget, money is definitely a consideration. The fellow will start coming around, fixing a bunch of small problems, such as installing new doorknobs or hanging a ceiling fan, and graduate to more complex tasks. That is when disillusionment sets in. During this early, honeymoon phase, however, I notice my wife's spirits brighten. She loves having workmen around the house, she loves watching their progress and learning their techniques, and she loves supervising them. She will chat them up during their breaks, and they will tell her the story of their lives. I will sometimes come down to the kitchen to see her fixing an omelet or a sandwich for these men, all in the name of bonding and getting the best possible work out of them. My daughter sometimes grumbles that her mom has forgotten her and me, and indeed I wonder what happened to *my* omelet. But overall, I am not jealous; I am glad that she seems so content.

The cast of characters keeps changing. There was Kenny, an elderly African American handyman from the South, who kept working partly to help support his grown children and grandchildren. He loved to talk about his gym workouts, and how strong he was for a man his age. There was Luis, a skillful Latino contractor who seemed to be on the run from the law, evading child support payments to two women. One day he simply stopped showing up, leaving his tools in our basement. There was Marcos, a hardworking Mexican with limited English, who grinned a lot. Each of them ended up costing me thousands of dollars—a little here, a little there—and each of them my wife swore by, until it turned out that they had botched some particular job that was just beyond their skill set and had to be redone. At this point my wife would become angry and wonder aloud why these goddamn men couldn't just admit that they didn't know how to do something, instead of botching it up. She would fulminate against the whole tribe of workmen, who so often did not show up when they promised, leaving her trapped in the house waiting futilely for their arrival. By inference, I sensed she was feeling disenchanted with the entire male sex—which happens to be my own gender placement, though I was completely blameless, for once.

I would try to console her. I would reassure her that the job would get done right in the course of time. It was as though my faithful wife had had a series of unhappy love affairs, and I, like a cuckolded husband, had had to assuage her sorrow after the breakups. Of course she denies that she has any romantic feelings towards these men, and thinks I am, as usual, making up fantasies in my head. I do live in my head, it's true, because my relationship to the physical, mechanical world is so attenuated.

Presently there are three workmen in the back, putting a new roof on the extension above our garden apartment. Our tenants have been suffering leaks in their bathroom during heavy rains. There is no question we need to undo the previous shoddy job and start all over again. Fortunately, the new head workman, a Ukrainian named Andy, seems extremely knowledgeable about roofing matters, if expensive. My wife is keeping an eye on him.

The Agnes Martin Retrospective

LAST WEEK I went to the Agnes Martin retrospective at the Guggenheim Museum. I had been wanting for weeks to go because I've always, always, always liked Martin's abstract paintings. I tried to talk my wife into going with me, since she is an ex-painter and admires Martin too, but she wanted to see it with one of her girlfriends so it was left to me to go alone. Just as well, since Martin's work is considered spiritual and contemplative, appropriate for a one-on-one communion. I had to find a hole in my schedule and finally one arose on a Friday, right after my annual medical examination. The news there was not great—my blood pressure numbers had gone up and I had gained weight, which my frowning internist told me were probably connected—but at least I could treat myself to this show of quiet paintings, which might reduce my stress.

Here I must digress and explain my attachment to abstract minimalist art. I grew up in the heyday of abstract expressionist and minimalist painting. My brother, an aspiring artist, studied with Ad Reinhardt, and he imbued me with an aesthetic of rigor and restraint, valuing above all internal consistency. From Rogier van der Weyden to Mark Rothko, everything had to be austere and profound. I remember going to the retrospective of Reinhardt paintings

76

at the Jewish Museum, where you were greeted with a list of items proscribed by the artist (no color, no drawing, etc.), until all that was left were these vertical canvases that looked completely black from a distance but revealed almost imperceptible divisions and markings up close. I really liked them. I suppose there was an element of pride in belonging to a cognoscenti who could appreciate such subtle refinements, but the bottom line was that I genuinely thrilled to this art. I liked Barnett Newman's paintings, which also looked darkly forbidding except for jagged drips in the middle, and Ellsworth Kelly's monochrome paint-box series, and Vija Celmins's all-gray wave fields. A high point of my lifelong museum-going experience was the Piet Mondrian retrospective at MoMA, where you could see up close the handmade lines that had traced the rectangles and cracks that time had wrought on the surfaces. So naturally I was a fan of Martin's austere, minimalist grids, though she disliked being labeled a minimalist and preferred to be called an abstract expressionist, the latter term regarded by her as more emotional, less intellectually based. She wanted people to feel her work deeply, not just cerebrally take it in.

There was some anxious talk among the critics that the Martin retrospective, which had originated to great acclaim at the Tate Modern in London, might suffer from the spiral configuration of the Guggenheim. Honestly, I have never understood this complaint that Frank Lloyd Wright's bowl-like architectural design fought with or ruined certain exhibits. Maybe I'm insensitive, but when I go to that museum I just look at each work in turn, the way I would if the building were a regular rectangle, and move on.

As is the Guggenheim's custom, the retrospective began near the ground level, with her earliest, student-like works on display; one was expected to walk arduously up the spiraling ramps, as though on one's knees in a religious pilgrimage, to reach finally her last paintings. In a spirit of rebelliousness, and to spare my leg muscles, I decided to do the opposite: take the elevator to the top floor and stroll downhill. Even if this meant having to reverse the narrative of her artistic career, from fruition to seed, why not run it backwards?

In her last paintings she had moved away from her celebrated black-gray-white palette into pastel shades, embracing sensuous, shimmering light effects. I wasn't sure what to make of this change. Some of these canvases were aglow, magical, while others verged on sentimental cotton candy. Artists in old age often loosen up, decoratively speaking: think of Willem de Kooning's final ribbon paintings. Martin had left the New York art world in 1967, traveled around the country, and settled in Taos, New Mexico, where she lived more or less like a hermit. She also abandoned art-making for a number of years, then took it up again, and eventually composed these pastel-shaded works, which still employed gridded or banded compositions. A wall statement informed the viewer that Martin, Zen-influenced, insisted all her work was about joy, happiness, and the love of this world. You could have fooled me. Her last pieces, however, suggested a conscientious working out of this "happiness" program—and seemed dubious for that reason. I worry when serious artists start telling me their purpose is to make me feel joy.

Moving to a lower incline, I found myself much more at ease with the gray paintings of the 1960s, with which I was already familiar. They featured meticulous graphite grids composed of thousands of patient strokes. Some of them I thought flat-out magnificent, while others just sat there mutely. I was baffled why one might seem so full and another empty, when both employed more or less the same technique. How would I begin to describe the difference? What specialist vocabulary would I need to appropriate, if called upon to write a review of the show? I thanked my lucky stars I was not an art critic. True, I had written a few pieces of art criticism in the past, and supposed I could do so again, if my back were against the wall financially. But I was at a loss for words when it came to making distinctions between the ones that worked for me and those that didn't. It may just have been I was accustomed to seeing only one or two Martins at a time, and there were so many here that I kept being sated and emptied out with distressing alacrity.

Much as I loved this middle period of Martin's work, I started feeling uneasy. All these tiny, fussy little parallel lines, what did they remind me of? Suddenly it came to me: a show I'd once seen of the outsider artist Martín Ramírez, who was a catatonic schizophrenic institutionalized in California mental hospitals. He built his beautiful drawings out of tiny repeated markings, compulsively. There was a clear relationship between his mental illness and his artistic style. The thought struck me then that maybe Martin was completely mad! All that talk about joy and happiness was the sign of someone who had to defend herself against powerful inner demons. Strangely enough, just as I was thinking this I came upon a wall placard mentioning that Martin had been schizophrenic, off and on, her entire life.

No wonder I was freaking out and wanting to leave the museum: I have always been leery around crazy people. Rightly or wrongly, I'm convinced I have a radar, a second sense, able to detect insanity in others. No doubt there's a certain amount of low-grade paranoid projection in this ostensible sensitivity; but however it operates, I continue absolutely to trust my instincts. For instance, I've had creative writing students who were, well, nuts. Ignoring my first impulse to flee during conference with them, I would discipline myself to sit quietly and listen to them babble for half an hour, and in the end we got along fine, the crazy ones and me.

This time, I was able to put aside my agitation and descend to the lower rungs of the Guggenheim, taking in the way Martin developed her strict mode of operation from early, tentative experiments. At every stage of her development, on every level of the Guggenheim, there had been some breathtaking pieces. It was, all in all, a show I was happy to have seen, and I left the museum feeling, by however minimal degrees, calmer.

Reflections After the Election

A WEEK HAS PASSED since the most disastrous United States election in memory. My first response was to feel sick—literally, to want to throw up. The repudiation of all one's most cherished humanistic, social justice, and planet-protecting values in one fell swoop cannot help but be taken personally. At least I took it personally. But I am starting to feel calmer. In that beneficent calm, may it continue a bit longer, I have been reflecting on certain errors or distortions in my thinking.

The first error had to do with relying overmuch on the damage ostensibly done by Donald Trump's racist, sexist, xenophobic, lying, or simply ignorant statements and actions. I would recite to myself his denigration of climate change explanations, his dissing of John McCain or the Khan family, his slandering of Mexicans as rapists and the Hispanic-heritage judge presiding over the Trump University case as biased, his taped boasting of forcing himself on women, his insistence that all the women who came forward to testify to his unwanted advances were liars, his virtually inviting someone on the NRA's side to shoot Hillary Clinton, his leading rallies in chants to "lock her up," his vowing to bring back torture or waterboarding, his mocking the disabled journalist, his outrageous promise to bar

Muslims from entering the country, or to build a wall on the border and make the Mexican government pay for it, or to deport two million undocumented immigrants, or to vacate treaties with our allies unless they paid a larger share of the bill, his refusal to accept the results if he lost, or to disclose his income tax records, and so on and so forth. These were my worry beads, which I counted every morning and evening. Surely, the accumulation of these bigoted, horrendous, un-civic positions, combined with the support of unsavory groups like the KKK for Trump, would result in his defeat. On the contrary: What I failed to take into account is that it is not a scandal if enough people refuse to find the seeming offense scandalous. All these could be waived, especially by voters who shared some of the same racist, sexist, bloodthirsty prejudices. Just so, these same Trump supporters were able to promote into odoriferous "scandals" what were really minor matters (see Hillary's connection to the Benghazi affair or her emails). Hence, the very nature of scandal was borne in on me as something much more fact-free and subject to manipulation than I had ever appreciated. Live and learn.

Again and again, Hillary Clinton appealed to Americans' higher nature—we are kinder, better, more tolerant, and so on—only to discover that many of her countrymen had no better natures. She would say "Love trumps hate"; it was all like a church sermon, and as often happens with sermons, it turned many voters off. It wasn't "fun." She was arguing that being president was serious business, we had to make the responsible decision, we couldn't turn the office over to someone who was an amateur in governance or give such an impulsive, intemperate, and self-serving individual the ultimate control over the nuclear button. Why not? said these voters.

The liberal-progressive commentators all blamed themselves

afterward for failing to take into sufficient account the "anger" of the "forgotten, disenfranchised" white working-class voters who had turned the tide. Now, anger is a very sexy notion for commentators to latch on to, but I think it has been overstated. I am sure it may have factored into some rural or working-class pockets in their decision to vote as they did, but given the fact that Barack Obama has rescued the economy from its deep recession and that millions of jobs have been added in the past eight years, and given the record of businessman Trump in stiffing American workers or campaigning against raising the minimum wage, it would seem puzzling that anger should be seen as the motivating factor swaying them to vote against their economic interests. Rather, I would say what mattered more was the desire to have fun, to be entertained, to do mischief and see chaos break out—what Mikhail Bakhtin called the "carnivalesque" turn. Electing a rogue who had never put in a day of public service in his life, who admitted to not paying taxes, was rather like the time the normally staid Minnesota voters swept the clearly unprepared ex-wrestler Jesse Ventura into the governor's house. Boredom and spite, more than righteous anger, were at the wheel. Dostoevsky's Underground Man argued that sometimes the only way to feel free is to spite our best interests.

And there is also the excitement of hating. In William Hazlitt's great essay "On the Pleasure of Hating," he wrote:

> Nature seems (the more we look into it) made up of antipathies: without something to hate, we should lose the very spring of thought and action. Life would turn to a stagnant pool, were it not ruffled by the jarring interests, the unruly passions, of men. The white streak in our own fortunes is brightened (or just rendered visible) by making

83

all round it as dark as possible; so the rainbow paints its form upon the cloud. Is it pride? Is it envy? Is it the force of contrast? Is it weakness or malice? But so it is, that there is a secret affinity, a *hankering* after evil in the human mind, and that it takes a perverse, but a fortunate delight in mischief, since it is a never-failing source of satisfaction. Pure good soon grows insipid, wants variety and spirit. Pain is a bitter-sweet, which never surfeits. Love turns, with a little indulgence, to indifference and disgust: hatred alone is immortal.

The dreaded Stephen Bannon's recommendation that Republicans needed to stoke up the hate in order to win the national election proved to be more realistic in the long run than Hillary's wishful slogan "Love Trumps Hate." Her advocacy of programs for women and children, minorities, and college students was seen as insipid, especially by white working-class males. Trump kept promising to *do* things for these disaffected working men, like bring back manufacturing and coal mining, and keep out the immigrants who might compete for these same jobs. So what if he could not reasonably accomplish any of these promises, at least he seemed to be addressing their concerns. Trump the mountebank paid them the compliment of pretending to have their interests at heart by conning them. Just as a woman will sometimes allow herself to be seduced by flattery she knows to be false, so the Rust Belt voters accepted Trump's empty promises as a minimal but necessary tribute, while probably suspecting in the end that nothing would change. Hillary, on the other hand, was too honest to promise what she could not deliver, and it cost her.

So I am back to counting my worry beads, but this time the litany is anticipatory. It goes something like: Suppose he appoints right-

REFLECTIONS AFTER THE ELECTION

wing judges and *Roe v. Wade* is nullified; suppose Obamacare is scrapped; suppose the international climate agreement is canceled and we accelerate the rate of pollution to the irreversible point; suppose Putin takes over Syria and Lithuania without a peep of protest from our president; suppose I have to look at Rudy Giuliani's ghoulish face for another four to eight years.... This list-making is not nearly as much fun as was the reiteration of Trump's boneheaded remarks, but anxiety requires that I keep doing so, if only as a superstitious primitive ritual to ward off evil by imagining it.

Letter from Shanghai

I AM IN CHINA, on a two-week visit during which I am expected to give four lectures at universities in Shanghai and Nanjing. This is my first time in Shanghai. The only other time I was in China, in 1990, I had been on a press junket to the film set of *Raise the Red Lantern*, in the countryside, and also spent a few days in Beijing. My lasting impressions were of myriad bicyclists and dust clouds from yellow earth swirling around. Sixteen years later, the bicyclists are mostly gone, replaced by cars and motorbikes that contribute mightily to the air pollution problem. Never mind the difficulty of crossing the street: moped drivers career through the sidewalks, ignoring the traffic laws and taking advantage of any opening, regardless of pedestrians. One is expected to scatter, which makes for a tense alertness on any walk around town. Then again, many university students resist walking at all because of the air pollution, preferring to take taxis, which are quite inexpensive. The only problem is that often cabbies are picky and refuse fares if it's to a section of town they want to avoid, which leads to the absurd situation of standing on a street corner for fifteen minutes trying to hail a cab in order to avoid pollution, while imbibing the sour-smelling, acrid air.

Shanghai, with a population of twenty-four million, is the largest city in China, possibly in the world, and it struck me as both exciting and gargantuan—overwhelming, in a word. My New York City seems small and cuddly by comparison. I've always been a fan of large cities—Cairo, Tokyo, Mexico City, Moscow, New York—but I may have met my match this time. Expecting a skyscraper cityscape, I was unprepared for the relentless superblock housing estates made of reinforced concrete, whose only regional touches are their pagoda-like pointed crowns. The Great Wall of China has been reborn in the form of these huge concrete mountain ranges that abut the highways. I suppose, given twenty-four million inhabitants, they are a realistic solution. Even with these units, Shanghai real estate remains among the priciest on the globe. The charming old neighborhoods with narrow streets that gave Shanghai its historical allure have been mostly razed to make way for these behemoths, punctuated by banal megamalls. You can still find pockets of turn-of-the-century or art deco streetscapes, but you have to search hard for them.

The construction frenzy has also drawn many of the world's star architects, who have contrived to pull apart the old Modernist box, like the Hulk bursting out of his jeans, with every imaginable curve, bulge, fold, and biomorphic extrusion: computer-generated novelties with light-show facades, hovering in one's judgment between amazement and distaste at their self-indulgent arbitrariness (then again, who said architecture had to be rigorously rational?), they are best seen at sundown from the Bund, Shanghai's famous promenade along the river, in all their garish splendor. I told myself I was seeing the future, the way people a hundred years ago used to think visiting New York City was getting a science-fiction preview.

I will close for now with two observations about Shanghai streets. First, there are these curious metal posts about three feet high on the edge of the curb that chatter away in Mandarin and English, telling you to get back behind the yellow line if they detect by sensors that you have strayed too far forward. Second, more benignly, there are strips of raised tile down the middle of the sidewalk, for the convenience of the blind.

Still in Shanghai

THE CLASS I'M TEACHING at Fudan University was thrown together during exam week, and the students seem to be there on a voluntary basis, so attendance is spotty. It meets three times, each session lasting two and a half hours, which is a lot of lecture time to fill. Unsure what level of English comprehension the students would have, I decided not to write out lectures but to improvise my talks. I requested, and was given, a translator, a white American named Isaac from Green Bay, Wisconsin, who has studied Mandarin for eight years. We are joined at the hip, I speaking a few sentences in English and he doing the best he can to put it into Chinese. Some of the students understand English well and are annoyed at this procedure, but others haven't a clue. The majority are linguistics majors. There are also a few auditors, professors from the biology and political science departments. I've had a hard time gauging the general level of literary sophistication, and sometimes I find myself mouthing platitudes like "You may be bored with yourself but you must find life interesting and a mystery." Where is this shit coming from? Desperation, mostly. I had mistakenly assumed I would be talking to creative writing graduate students, only to learn no creative writing courses were offered at this university. They are expected to write only academic papers, sometimes six per course, and could use some help, they say, in that area, like the very bright student who is writing a thesis on Wallace Stevens and reading Heidegger. They seem puzzled at my championing the personal essay and urging the employment of subjectivity, contrarianism, and expressiveness in forming a style. One student told me flat out: "In China there is no such thing as the personal essay."

I know this isn't strictly true because I included a few examples from the writer Lu Xun in my *Art of the Personal Essay* anthology. Lu Xun (1881–1936) is revered as one of the greatest modern Chinese writers. His largely autobiographical sketches about impoverished intellectuals or the hardships of common people have a forlorn poignancy and admirable directness. I decided to make a pilgrimage to his house and the nearby Lu Xun Park, with its mausoleum and museum. We have been incredibly fortunate, my wife and I, in being assigned a succession of English-speaking student guides who not only negotiate all dealings with taxi drivers, ticket sellers, waiters, and merchants but insist on paying for everything (as their dean has instructed them). These young graduate students are kind, open, resourceful, and wonderfully attentive. Pointless to generalize about a people, especially one as numerous as the Chinese, but I have to say that those we've encountered on this trip have been extraordinarily hospitable; they put Americans to shame by comparison in our care of foreign visitors.

The neighborhood where Lu Xun spent his last years is a well-preserved area of stucco villas, alleys, and sturdy old houses covered in alternating gray and orange brick striations, topped with orange tiled roofs—a welcome remnant of old Shanghai. The author's narrow three-story house, as it happened, was closed for repairs; it stood at the end of a cul-de-sac alley, and we were fine with viewing it from the outside.

We walked on to Lu Xun Park, which was a lively public space, with several competing bands playing simultaneously, à la Charles Ives. There were also knots of oldsters singing nostalgically the songs of their youth. I had gotten the misimpression from hanging around the university area that China was a country of the young. So this was where they were keeping the old people!

Inside the park, the Lu Xun Museum, a large modern building, beckoned. Its exhibits featured photographs of the handsome if grimly stern author, his two wives, his friends and teachers, as well as his manuscripts and letters, and a wall of book jackets from various editions of his work in China and around the world. I could not help envying the way this author was honored, and was unable to think of a single American writer accorded the same respectful treatment. On the other hand, I was put off by the way the poor guy had been co-opted by the Chinese Communist Party after his death and turned into a proto-Maoist saint. The CCP needed heroes, and he fit the bill, though he never joined the Party during his lifetime and was jealously protective of his independence. I asked our student guide, an intelligent, tactful young woman, whether she agreed with this assessment. She said it was common knowledge that he had been used by the Party for propaganda purposes, but that everyone was free to read him and draw their own conclusions.

Hesitant to probe her political views further, which might land her in trouble, I let it drop. We ended the excursion by stopping at a hole-in-the-wall takeout joint that we were told made the best soup dumplings (a Shanghai specialty) in town. They were indeed absolutely delicious.

On to Nanjing

THOSE WHO HAVE BEEN FOLLOWING this blog know that for the last ten days my wife and I have been in China, a combination of work and pleasure. Most of the time we were in Shanghai, but we also took a day trip to Suzhou, famous for its elaborate gardens. There we toured the smaller one, the Lion Grove, with its stones twisted into grotesque baroque shapes, and the Humble Administrator's Garden, which, despite its title, is quite grand. Part of what makes it so is the progression from indoor pavilions (with poetic names like Pavilion for Listening to the Sound of the Rain) to picturesque ponds and waterfalls: the landscape contracted and expanded like an accordion. It is Nature Orchestrated, able to accommodate crowds without any compromise of its picturesque beauty, much the way Frederick Law Olmsted's Central Park and Prospect Park do, and I wondered if he drew on them for inspiration.

We also were taken to a restaurant on the canal in Suzhou where, in a private upstairs room, I ate one of the best meals in my life. Though we have consistently dined well in China, I had a few meals where the food was prepared so exquisitely, so delicately, that I ascended to an empyrean realm and became at long last a foodie. If I were merely to list the names of the dishes, it would not tell you much, since they were largely the same we encountered in other, more banal banquets, or for that matter, in Chinese restaurants stateside. The difference was more in the freshness of ingredients and the subtlety and skill of their preparation.

In Nanjing, I met up with my friend Huang Fan, who had invited me to China. Huang is a brilliant poet, an omnivorous reader, and a professor of literature and visual arts. He dresses in a uniform that rarely varies: khaki t-shirt, jeans, and military cap, an ironic tribute to his youthful dislike of the army. The first night, I gave a reading of my work and was heartened to see the overflow crowd of students and locals (thanks to Huang's publicity efforts). The question and answer session that followed the reading was so enthusiastic that I sensed the audience's enormous appetite for literature in general and American culture in particular. When it finally ended, with many hands still raised, a crowd swarmed the front with requests to be photographed with me. Selfies are big in China, and for one evening I was allowed to feel like a rock star.

In the sightseeing days that have followed (with Huang's wife at the wheel, since he doesn't drive), I've been struck by what a gracious, leafy, lovely city Nanjing is. Of course it's much smaller than Shanghai, only (only!) eight million inhabitants, roughly the population of New York City. Much of the original low-scale environment has been permitted to stand, as well as the shade trees that line many streets and form a canopy. Some of these old trees have been pruned and trained to stand uptight, at parade attention. There are forests in the middle of the city; the countryside never feels far away. The same dreary housing estates and megamalls I saw in Shanghai can be found here, but they're mainly set on the outskirts.

Huang took me to an impressive bookstore, Librairie Avant-Garde, which occupied what had once been an underground garage. The floor tilted upward in the middle and a car was impishly parked inside, to pay homage to its former life. On the walls were posters of international literary heroes such as Samuel Beckett, Jorge Luis Borges, Pier Paolo Pasolini, Susan Sontag, Walter Benjamin. Table after table was covered with rigorously highbrow titles, including lots of contemporary American authors such as Paul Auster, Cormac McCarthy, and Lydia Davis, and French theorists such as Pierre Bourdieu, Michel Foucault, and Roland Barthes, as well as the world's classics and ancient Greek, Roman, and Chinese texts. The film selection carried books on every conceivable cutting-edge direc- tor. Throughout the store mostly young people were reading or typing on their laptops, so that it looked like a combination library, study hall, and bookstore. I was floored by the air of intellectual seriousness, as well as the absence of the merchandise (tchotchkes, nonbooks) that our chain bookstores sell. It seemed that China was much less closed off to the world than I'd imagined. Perhaps only books that directly criticized the Communist Party and the present regime were censored, though that made for a significant gap.

I saw the other side of the coin when Huang's wife had to return to her office (she works in a publishing firm that will soon be releas- ing two of my books in translation) to practice a group sing of the new Chinese Communist Party anthem. Her company will be forced to compete with several others on July 1st, an important CCP anniversary, for the best rendition, and participation is mandatory, from the company director on down. She refused to sing it in the car for us, having already done it ten times that day, but played it on her cell phone. I then held forth with a lusty if truncated version of "The East Is Red." Huang and his wife were astonished that I knew it. I explained that my generation, which was so fervently against the U.S. government during the Vietnam War, had for a long time idealized Mao, the Little Red Book, "the wind from the East," and so on, before we learned about the millions who perished in the famine and the Cultural Revolution.

"And now what do you think of Mao?" Huang asked.

"I think he's one of the three worst killers in history. Stalin, Mao, Hitler."

The car got rather silent.

"And what do you think of your country now?" Huang responded.

"I feel much warmer toward my country, though I know it's made plenty of mistakes."

In 1990, the first time I visited China (shortly after the Tiananmen Square massacre), I couldn't detect any enthusiasm for the Communist Party among the film crowd I spoke to; and I sensed on this trip that many Chinese artists and intellectuals lived a kind of internal exile, cautiously silent in public and thinking heretical thoughts in private. For me, the current trip has been marked by paradox. I've been feeling a tremor of fear that never quite leaves, in the face of an authoritarian regime that censors the internet and throws dissidents in jail if they cross a shifting line, and at the same time I'm experiencing waves of affection for the Chinese people themselves: their endurance, their culture, their humanity.

The Paradox of Urban Density

THE OLDER I GET, the less sure I become about certain pet ideas I had thought were written in stone. Part of this uncertainty comes from my tendency to want to turn my convictions upside down, just for the fun of seeing the other side, but another part has to do with the way history and time yield unexpected kinks in my belief system. Lately I've been thinking about urban density: Is it a good or bad thing?

In the late nineteenth and early twentieth centuries, with Jacob Riis's *How the Other Half Lives* exposing the abysmal living conditions of tenement dwellers in New York's Five Points district and Lower East Side, and the recurrent plagues of infectious diseases that would sweep through the slums, killing off hundreds if not thousands, a consensus arose that tightly jammed-together dwellings for immigrants and poor people were an evil that needed to be corrected. The buildings were seen as pestilential in themselves, lacking in sunlight and ventilation and thus miasmic, to use the term then in circulation. Legislation was passed to ensure that new tenements would have to allow for windows open to the sun and air shafts. But the slums remained slums, so social reformers began clamoring for these ramshackle districts to be demolished and replaced by more modern hygienic structures.

The upshot, starting with the New Deal and continuing into the postwar era, was an ambitious, federally funded urban renewal program, which engaged in slum clearance and replaced the old tenements with high-rise public housing. These "projects" have been so roundly disparaged, most notably from Jane Jacobs's 1961 *The Death and Life of Great American Cities* onward, that we sometimes forget they sprang from idealistic motives to improve the living conditions of the poor. Many of the initial residents rejoiced at the chance to move into clean, modern apartments, and in fact the waiting lists for vacancies in New York projects continue to be long, given the city's shortage of affordable housing. If the social reformers seemed to follow the towers in the park schema recommended by Le Corbusier, it was not because they were so enamored of that quirky Swiss-French architect's urbicidic vision but because they were trying to bring down the density figures in these neighborhoods by providing enough grass and public space between the high-rise buildings—enough sun and air.

But Jacobs had been right to criticize the loss of community feeling, as retail stores were eliminated and the foot-traffic pleasures of urban encounter curtailed by projects that seemed to turn their backs on the street. Jacobs also took aim at the proponents of garden cities, who hoped to reduce urban noise and visual clutter by decentralizing strategies that would build new, orderly communities and siphon off some of the big cities' population. (Examples of such experiments actually built include Radburn, New Jersey; Sunnyside Gardens, Queens; and Seaside, Florida.)

Here we come to a basic semantic conflict: The garden city champions, such as Ebenezer Howard, Patrick Geddes, Clarence Stein, and Lewis Mumford, employed the word *congestion* with its negative connotation, arguing that some limits should be set on the demographics per acre, while the anti–garden city followers of Jacobs preferred the more neutral term *density*.

I, being a lover of big cities, crowds, and the hurly-burly spectacle of street life, was a total Jacobs follower. I saw no reason to "tidy up" the city or thin out its population. I scoffed at New Town propaganda like *The City*, a WPA documentary short by Ralph Steiner that showed the lunch-hour masses thronging the streets of New York as if this were something to be appalled instead of excited by, followed by shots of happy children on tricycles circling suburban lawns. The assumption of the New Towners seemed to be that big-city density reduced the individual to an ant or an automaton—which concept I rejected because it was not true to my experience. America had long suffered from this sort of anti-urban bias, and I was having none of it.

In recent decades, an interesting turnabout has occurred. Suddenly, density began to be embraced by city planners. It was decoupled from prior identification with slums; swanky Park Avenue apartment houses, it was pointed out, had some of the highest densities in the country. Greenwich Village, the neighborhood Jacobs had held up as an exemplar of good urban living, had the same density as Pruitt–Igoe, the St. Louis housing project that had been seen as an abject failure and dynamited. Moreover, with global warming becoming an increasing worry, urban density seemed positively ecological, as it required a smaller electric grid, used up less energy than exurban sprawl, took less of a bite out of agricultural land and forests, and made mass transportation a more viable option.

"Infill" became a rallying cry: closing the gaps in the city's fabric with new construction, rather than spreading out farther by amalgamating—swallowing up—smaller municipalities at the borders.

For a while, I was perfectly contented, even smug, to be on the winning side of the congestion/density debate. But then I started to wonder about some of the downsides of density, especially with megalopolises. There are now ten cities around the world with a population of more than fifteen million, and fifteen cities with a population of more than ten million. In some of these metropolises, such as New Delhi and Beijing, the air pollution is so severe that schools are closed for days at a time and children told to stay indoors. Enormous traffic jams choke the roads. In Shanghai, which I visited recently, there were seemingly unending walls of high-rise housing estates, because with a population estimated between twenty-four and twenty-eight million, you're going to need a lot of apartments. Even given the new construction, Shanghai real estate is scandalously expensive. Land prices being so inflated, the first neighborhoods to be wiped out were the older, traditional, low-rise ones. With them went a good deal of the charm and historical memory of the city.

I find myself thinking, heretically: Maybe Howard, Geddes, Mumford, and Stein had a point when they argued that some limits should be placed on population growth so that a city might continue to be, well, livable. Then again, livable is itself a moving target, capable of being continuously revised and readjusted depending on circumstance. Maybe the hour has passed when such density restrictions could even be enforced—in which case, garden cities might turn out to be an attractive temporary solution. Or should we say, as the experts do, that there is "good density" and "bad density" and leave it at that? It's all too complicated for me to figure out.

Father-in-Law

I'VE BEEN MARRIED TWICE, but have only had to deal with one father-in-law. In my first marriage, undertaken when I was twenty, my wife Carol had a strong if ambivalent connection to her father, Paul, who was a Viennese psychoanalyst. My present wife, Cheryl, had a runaway father: once he'd divorced her mother, he disappeared from his daughter's life, a sad development for her, but that meant by the time I met her and proposed, I did not have to live up to another father-in-law's stringent standards.

My first and only father-in-law, Paul, was a romantic figure—or at least his daughter romanticized him, as did I. He had escaped the Nazis by fleeing the country when he saw soldiers with swastikas in front of his building. A Jewish graduate student in German literature, he left behind the love of his life. In a displaced persons camp he met Ellen, the woman who would become his wife: not that he had strong feelings for her, but she was a decent, sensible woman who adored him and she would do. They both came to the United States, where his sponsor convinced him to switch professions, and he went into training as a psychoanalyst in Topeka, Kansas. The family—which by now consisted of Paul, Ellen, and their two daughters, Carol and her younger sister, Barbara—moved to Bethesda, Maryland, just outside Washington, D.C., when he was offered a job at the National Institute of Mental Health. There he engaged in research while seeing private patients in his suburban home.

The whole family had accustomed themselves to being silent while he was seeing patients. Some of that silence persisted even after the patients had gone; the feeling I got was that everything in the household revolved around this melancholy man's taciturn mood. He seemed to me almost a parody of a German professor: pipe-smoking, listening to the classical music station, picking up and reading a professional journal in his armchair, only to lay it down irritably for one of several books on the coffee table, a little stiff in his manner, not a chatterbox, you had to instigate the conversation each time and hope to engage him.... I learned through others that he was something of an eclectic freethinker when it came to psychotherapeutic practice, and I would have liked to quiz him about his departure from standard Freudianism, but he was not forthcoming on professional matters. I sensed he regarded native-born Americans as childish, naive, and intellectually primitive. He also had, like Theodor Adorno, that European snobbishness toward American popular culture, and grumbled about the poor quality of American bread. I was fascinated by him, as if I were encountering one of Thomas Mann's characters in real life. Though I mocked him behind his back, I desperately wanted his approval. That was not to be: he was one of those people who draws others to him by withholding his approval, just a little, just enough to keep you believing it might be possible....

His younger daughter, Barbara, resisted his somber air and clowned around; he loved her mischievous sassiness, craved its lightness. But Carol, my wife, was more the thoughtful, sad type, like him: she kept getting pulled into his dark, heavy orbit, hoping for his approval by shining academically. When she was a teenager, he had used her at times as his library assistant, fetching books. Precisely because he identified with her, he worried that she was in for a troubled life. He had a way of making her doubt herself. Then she met me and started to break away from his influence. I encouraged her to rebel against him. We were enacting that typical pattern of a first love that allows two young people to distance themselves from their parents.

But I myself was drawn to him—physically and mentally. He was a good-looking man with a masculine, character-filled face, somewhat like the actor Paul Henreid; a full head of hair, big shoulders, and strong hands, and he liked to wear plaid woolen shirts. He had that typically Tyrolean appetite for hiking, mountains, and the outdoors. The family always took camping vacations, something I never did when I was growing up. I came from a Brooklyn slum, essentially a ghetto, and I think he was put off by both my working-class manner and my obvious Jewishness. A secular humanist, he downplayed his religion—the kind of Jew who tells his children once and only once that they are Jewish so that they will know in case the Gestapo comes again.

As for the whole bourgeois suburban setup, so foreign to me, I was both enchanted and repelled by it. The house had so many rooms that everyone was always going off into their own sanctuary; it was too quiet, too lonely. I did like the comfortable couch, the spacious living room, the backyard whose trees concealed next-door neighbors from view. But my impulse was to hide in the basement, which I did even for part of our wedding party, avoiding as much as possible the living room filled with Paul's colleagues who were strangers to me.

It was shortly after the ceremony that Paul took me by the arm and said, "I know you want to be a writer. In every century there are maybe three writers who count. In the nineteenth century, it was Goethe, Balzac, and Tolstoy. In the twentieth century, Proust, Joyce, maybe Kafka or Rilke. If it doesn't work out, you can always do something with television or advertising. I have complete faith in you." Meaning, he had faith that I would give up this impractical dream and decide to make money. I think he saw me (rightly, it turned out) as an unreliable provider. At the time I was deeply offended. Now that I'm the father of a young woman who is dating boys lacking in maturity, I can see it makes sense that he might worry about this long-haired wannabe writer's ability to take care of his daughter. He kept inquiring when we were planning to get health insurance. At twenty-one, who bothers about health insurance? Ridiculous, right? Now I know better.

Surely, there was competitiveness between us over literature. He had been a professor of German literature, after all. His letters to his daughter were filled with quotes from Goethe, Schiller, Hölderlin, and Novalis. He had precise handwriting, he used a fountain pen with green ink, and there would always be indented lines of poetry, half a stanza, let's say, in German. I would get Carol to translate them for me, then I would make fun of him: it seemed so pompous to write your daughter that way, with little wisdom nuggets from classical German poets. Still, the fact that he had committed all these poems to memory was impressive, I had to admit.

In one of his letters he said with a sigh that he spent an hour every day reading literature, and often he was disappointed. I thought this was the most asinine thing I had ever heard. Who was he to be disappointed with literature? I worshipped at the shrine of literature;

it could never fail me. I mean, I understand now that he saw patients during the day, and at night, tired, he would pick up a novel or a book of poetry and ... well, okay, he was disappointed, I get it. He had a right to be disappointed. But we were coming from such different places. One time when he was reading James Baldwin's *Another Country*, the season's most praised, he patted the book and said with approving solemnity, "This man has known suffering." I wanted to laugh out loud. From my sampling of the book, I thought *Another Country* corny and contrived—still do, in fact. I love Baldwin's essays, less so his novels. Regardless: it was Paul's willingness to be so touched by this African American writer that resonated in me long after, in retrospect. At the time, though, I was the sworn enemy of solemnity.

A few years later, Carol and I were at a film festival in Montreal when we received a phone message: Paul had died of a massive heart attack on a camping trip. We rushed to the burial. It was not long after that our marriage broke up. Perhaps my father-in-law had been keeping us together all this time by the force of his disapproval.

James Baldwin, Prophet vs. Writer

ONE OF THE MOST highly touted movies of this past year has been Raoul Peck's documentary about James Baldwin, *I Am Not Your Negro*. Being a longtime lover of Baldwin's prose, I snatched at the invitation to a press screening. While his first two novels, *Go Tell It on the Mountain* and *Giovanni's Room*, are capable efforts, I am much more captivated by his essays, which seem to me miraculous, magical achievements. Quite simply, I regard him as one of America's two or three greatest essayists. So I was especially curious to see this film, which purported to be based on an unfinished book, discovered in Baldwin's papers, about three assassinated African American leaders he had known: Medgar Evers, Malcolm X, and Martin Luther King Jr.

I say "purported," because the fragmented text, or set of notes, is used as a hook at the beginning (we hear a few passages read aloud by Samuel L. Jackson) and soon disappears, giving way to a mash-up of quotes from other more familiar works of his, footage from his public appearances, and news clips of recent racial troubles. Peck, a skillful veteran filmmaker, has put together a worthy introduction to Baldwin for the general public. Of course I should not have been surprised that there was nothing new here for me, nor was it reasonable for me to have expected a commercial motion picture to engage closely with a written text, and yet the archivist in me was disappointed.

Baldwin is as ever a kinetic, charismatic presence on-screen, his mobile facial expressions signaling shades of intelligence, qualification, and nuance as he fields the questions by denser interviewers or eloquently rebuts statements by blustering fellow panelists. His dark suit, white shirt, and thin black tie (the preferred uniform of sixties jazz musicians) have an elegance and dignity that complement his half-boyish, half-worldly grin or smoldering looks of outrage. That's the given. The problem, for me, is that Jimmy the public figure begins to subsume Baldwin the writer. As he became famous, he was sought after to explain to white audiences the reasons why Black people were fed up or rioting, and he gave in to a pundit's warnings and prognostications. By juxtaposing Baldwin's rhetorical pronouncements with footage of recent police carnage and African American unrest, Peck is essentially freezing him in the role of prophet and making him the posthumous "witness" and spokesman for our current racial malaise.

There are two aspects that need to be considered here: 1) How good a prophet was he, in fact? 2) What effect might this public persona have had on the quality of his writing in the second half of his life? In addressing the first question, I find many of his predictions overblown. The revolutionary apocalypse overturning white America, which he predicted in *The Fire Next Time*, did not come to pass nor—given the resiliency of the U.S. capitalist system, like it or not—is it apt to occur now. He also tended to make dubious statements, such as accusing white people of being responsible for the death of Malcolm X, or saying that whites are lacking in the sexual spontaneity department, to which I would respectfully demur. We do him no favors as a thinker to accept unquestioningly every statement he made. He has certainly become a useful heroic symbol for expressing our contemporary dismay at the persistence of racism, and a corrective to American complacency, and perhaps that should be enough. But being preoccupied with the essay form, I can't help wanting to understand better his arc as an essayist. The film, by running together quotes of his writing at different stages without distinguishing their dates of composition, made Baldwin out to be always in command, a consistent oracular figure, not subject to the vicissitudes and blockages of every writer.

I felt reluctant to state aloud my reservations about the film, especially to those who loved it. Then I came upon a recent review by James Campbell in *The Times Literary Supplement*, which expressed similar misgivings. Campbell, a Scotsman, had written a superb biography of Baldwin; he'd had personal dealings with the writer as his editor and knew the man's story inside out. In addition to questioning the film's title credit "Written by James Baldwin," which he thought would have been better characterized as "Script derived from texts by...," and pointing out the uncomfortable fact, never mentioned in the movie, that MLK had distanced himself from Baldwin because of the latter's homosexuality, he made this bold assessment:

> The assassination of his three heroes caused a rupture in Baldwin's nervous system and stalled the flow of ink in his prose. "I didn't know for a long time whether I wanted to keep writing or not," he said later. "What I said to myself was that Martin never stopped. So I can't either." In fact, he published many books after 1968, but the

fluent prose of his early essays, incorporating memoir and moral philosophy—the prose of "Notes of a Native Son," "Equal in Paris," "The Black Boy Looks at the White Boy" (about his relationship with Norman Mailer), "Down at the Cross" and others—was gone. It had been sustained by a morale based on the belief that "we, human beings, can be better than we are." The bullet that killed King riddled that morale and put the validity of optimism in question.

Now, I agree completely with Campbell's assertion that Baldwin's writing after 1968 lost its magic. I just think he's giving him too noble an excuse in saying the diminishment occurred because he was disillusioned by the world's violence. Nor does Baldwin really need an excuse for his books falling off in quality: even the finest writers frequently do not sustain their best efforts over a lifetime. That's not a shame, nor a scandal, but the most normal thing in the world, especially for a writer like Baldwin, whose early gift was akin to that of a lyric poet; and we all know that lyric poets tend to burn out once they hit middle age. In his later years Baldwin kept accepting advances for book projects that he couldn't complete; he procrastinated, not necessarily from a response to American racism (he had been living in Europe at that point for quite a while), and those projects he did complete often ended up digressive messes with some beautiful passages scattered here and there. Such dogged if doomed efforts in the face of artistic decline have their own heroic dimension. *I Am Not Your Negro* does not come close to touching that drama, but its inclusion, in my opinion, would have made for a more interesting or at least more honest movie.

Marrying a Widow

THOSE WHO MARRY a widow may find themselves competing with a ghost. Such has been my experience. It started with a joke. Years ago, after a series of amorous misfires, I said to my friend Sally, half in jest, "The divorcées are bitter, and the women who have never married are bitter. What I really need to find is a widow, who loved her husband and therefore may retain some fondness for men."

Sally said, "I do know a widow. She's pretty, intelligent, artistic, and still in her thirties."

She introduced me to Cheryl, who had been married to a painter named Edward Flood. Cheryl had met Edward when she was eighteen, he thirty-one. In photographs, he appears as a tall, skinny, broad-shouldered guy with a mop of curly hair: I can see the attraction. They went out for a number of years, and both moved to New York where they lived together at the edge of poverty in a loft in Williamsburg. Though Edward was a gifted artist, he wasn't selling much at this point, so he supported himself occasionally as an adjunct instructor, more often as a skilled carpenter and construction hand. He also did what artists were supposed to do in those days, which was to smoke cigarettes and drink a lot. That, plus the harmful chemicals that painters inhaled then, may have led to his contracting brain cancer. Cheryl took him for medical treatments, but it was already too late. She decided they should get married, to demonstrate their love and perhaps enact superstitiously a defiant faith that he could be cured. Her mother was opposed to her marrying Edward, rather understandably, because he was a penniless artist and dying; but Cheryl ignored her, being fully in the throes of a romantic gesture. They were married only a couple of months when he passed away, at age forty-one.

A widow still in her twenties, she struggled to sort out his artistic estate, managed to get an exhibition, and put the rest in storage. Several years passed under a cloud of grief. She had just begun to get back in the dating game when I met her. She was, as promised, attractive, sensitive, intelligent, with good moral values, but somber and pessimistic. Slowly I convinced her that we could have a future together. I sensed she was not passionately in love with me, as she had been with Edward, but that was all right: I'm uncomfortable as an object of adoration. Her friends counseled her that she should grab the chance, and so she did, suspecting that if she did not I would soon move on to another potential childbearing wife.

It took her some getting used to, living with a character like me. I was so unlike Edward: because they were both visual artists, they could understand each other on a nonverbal level, and they shared the same interest in the art world and the same bohemian lifestyle, whereas I insisted on putting everything in words and was much more drawn to bourgeois security. When we quarreled, I suspected that she wished she were still with her first love.

I took to referring to Edward banteringly as her "real husband." I played up this idea of my being merely a substitute, partly to extract a denial from her and partly to diffuse my own jealousy by exaggerating it. There is a funny riff in Jean Renoir's film *La Chienne* where the harridan of a wife keeps comparing her present husband disdainfully to her sainted late husband, whose portrait she keeps above the mantel. Three-quarters through the movie, we learn that the first husband hadn't died but had simply run away. Cheryl was disinclined to make comparisons between us, but I sometimes got her to talk about Edward, their trips to Mexico, his refusal to have children. It came out that life with Edward was not all roses. He too had a somber streak, and when he got angry he would refuse to speak for days. I may have many faults as a husband, but my pouts rarely last beyond a day. And Cheryl, for her part, would no longer put up with such treatment. If I start to sulk, she will immediately scoff, "Oh, so now you're giving us the silent treatment? Don't be such a baby!"

I have also, I like to think, taught her to laugh. When we first got together, she was, as mentioned, morose and pessimistic. Over the years she has become someone who frequently jokes, laughing at herself and more inclined to merriment.

Every year, as widows do, she'd get a little sad around the season of her first husband's death. But the birth of our child made her transfer the bulk of those emotions to Lily, and Edward became more of an afterthought. After twenty-six years of marriage, I recognize that she loves me as much as if not more than she ever did Edward, though in a different way, and is happy or content to be my wife. If anything, I am the one who has kept the romance of Edward alive in my head, as a tantalizing irritant. He, the promising artist who died young, and I, the schlemiel who shovels out several hundred dollars a month to the storage company to house his artworks. "Why can't we just ship it off to his relatives in Colorado?" I would ask. She'd reply, "Because they don't value art and never understood his becoming an artist. They'd probably toss it all in the garbage."

Recently, Cheryl arranged for two gallery shows of her late husband's work in Chicago. The first sold fairly well, the second not at all. I am resigned to never recouping the money I've spent on Edward's storage—or should I say "storing Edward," my spectral predecessor. We do have some of his art hung on our walls, and it doesn't bother me. I think I would actually miss them if they were someday taken down.

Memories of Jazz Nights

A FEW NIGHTS AGO I was at Dizzy's Club in New York's Lincoln Center, listening to the Fahir Atakoglu Trio, a Turkish modern jazz group. A friend invited me and since I had not yet been to Dizzy's (suspicious of anything to do with Wynton Marsalis, that affable mediocre popularizer), it seemed a good idea. The music was lively, complex, driving, an intriguing blend of John Coltrane/McCoy Tyner harmonics and a more dirgelike Istanbul sound, the room was comfortable with great views of the city, and I wondered why I had stopped going to hear live jazz when I always used to enjoy it so much.

In my youth I had spent a lot of time in jazz clubs. I started going to them when I was fifteen and, being underage—they checked your ID at the door—I borrowed a photocopied birth certificate from a friend of mine who was eighteen and Black, hoping that the gate-keepers would not look too closely at the box marked "race." From the late 1950s through the mid-1960s, I was mad about jazz, but then so was everybody. Jazz encapsulated the downbeat quality of the streets in New York's gritty, pre-boom, black-and-white era. When John Cassavetes made his first, improvisatory film, *Shadows*, starting in 1956, you knew he just had to have Charles Mingus on the soundtrack to accompany Ben Carruthers walking aimlessly around Times Square.

Still in high school, I listened late at night to the jazz deejays on the radio, Symphony Sid and Mort Fega. It was one of jazz's golden ages: You had the innovators, like Coltrane, Ornette Coleman, Thelonious Monk, Mingus, Eric Dolphy, Sun Ra, Sonny Rollins, and Cecil Taylor; and there were still a lot of great musicians around from the swing and bop eras, Roy Eldridge, Coleman Hawkins, and Benny Carter, not to mention Duke Ellington, Count Basie, and Louis Armstrong; and then there were the hard boppers, Horace Silver, Johnny Griffin, Gene Ammons, and Art Blakey, who weren't particularly groundbreaking but could swing like crazy. "Finger Poppin'" was the title of a Silver tune, and though I thought it might be a bit shallow, I couldn't keep from jumping up and down whenever Symphony Sid played it.

Most of the jazz clubs I frequented were in and around Greenwich Village: the Jazz Gallery on St. Mark's Place, the Five Spot around the corner on Cooper Square, the Half Note on Hudson Street, the Village Vanguard on Seventh Avenue, and the Village Gate on Bleecker Street. I would take the subway downtown from Columbia and wait in line at the Jazz Gallery, along with the hipsters, the hookers in furs, and the European tourists, and sometimes one of the Termini brothers, Joe or Iggy, who owned the club and rumor had it were mob-connected (but good guys, because supportive of jazz as their legit business/tax write-off), would be out there counting the house. I often went by myself, drinking deeply and pleasurably from the bluesy well of loneliness, as only adolescents can. I remember one night, waiting for Monk to come on; I was pissed off that it was two a.m. and he still hadn't arrived, while some Swedish tourists happily accepted the delay as part of the show. Finally Monk took the stage, played a few notes, hopped off and did a jig, sat back on the piano stool, and carried on erratically for forty-five minutes. Genius he undoubtedly was, but strange, possibly insane.

In those days I could stay up late, till two, three, four in the morning, and then greet the Greenwich Village dawn on Eighth Street. That's one reason I stopped going to clubs: around ten thirty it starts to be my bedtime now. But then, I had stamina: I could sit through two sets at least. When I started dating young women, I would take them to hear Coltrane, my favorite. It was a test: if they hid out in the bathroom because they found it too loud, that put the kibosh on any future romance. Coltrane *was* loud, and he was Serious Business. Exploding through "My Favorite Things," he looked like a high priest, and when you sat listening to him you were hitched to his spiritual journey, or maybe it was his ordeal, blowing the lid off a tune, tormented or ecstatic, it was hard to tell. Just before he died, when he started pounding his chest onstage like an ape, I began to fear for his sanity as well.

There were some tense moments between these African American jazz giants and the largely white crowd that had come to hear them. One night I trekked all the way to the farthest reaches of Queens in a snowstorm to catch Mingus and his quintet. There were about twenty people, all Mingus devotees, hardy souls who had weathered the snow, and Mingus, who had a temper, started tearing into us— us!—because the turnout was so small. What was wrong with this country that it failed to honor its one great indigenous art form, etc., etc. Years later I saw him again, playing to a full house of mostly Japanese tourists: He had a band of about twenty—an orchestra, really—and he was handing out sheet music to the musicians who were clearly willing but hadn't had much chance to practice together.

His scores had gotten increasingly complex, symphonic, and the poor musicians were scratching their heads trying to keep up.

Jazz musicians are often playing for each other, as how could they not be, flashing appreciative grins at a fellow player's felicitous lick. I once saw Dolphy, with that unicorn-like bone protruding from his forehead, already a star headliner at the Five Spot, hurrying to the Jazz Gallery when his set was over to sit in with Coltrane, pushing their new music further. Another time, I was at a Sunday-afternoon concert in a Harlem high-school auditorium, listening to the trumpeter Freddie Hubbard and the tenor saxophonist Booker Ervin, when near the end of the performance Dolphy rushed down the aisle, joyously hopping onstage to join them, though he hadn't been listed to appear. It seemed he knew about the gig and just wanted to be part of it.

I have many wonderful memories from that era of going to hear jazz. So why did I stop doing it? Well, I was never good at hanging out, and I suppose the late-night hours, the cover charges, and the seediness of these clubs eventually wore on me. But the bigger reason was that many of my favorite musicians died all at once, and with their passing, the music changed. Coltrane died, Dolphy died, Monk died, and Hawkins, Eldridge, Dinah Washington. I tried to keep up, going to hear what was left of the Coltrane group, Pharoah Sanders and Alice Coltrane, or Joe Henderson, but it wasn't the same, didn't have the same intensity. Or *I* didn't have the same intensity, the same need. I had left bohemianism behind. So I settled into playing my jazz records (now transferred to CDs) at home and, once in a blue moon, going to a club for old times' sake. I still love to listen to the way a musician will, on a good night, build a solo, phrase by phrase, and strike fire in the midst of that technical craft.

Listening to Dinah: "Don't Explain"

I AM LISTENING to Dinah Washington sing "Don't Explain." She is telling her man she knows he is cheating on her. Despite the lyric's insistence that she still loves him and it doesn't matter, her voice is harsh, bitter, weary. Disillusioned. She is basically saying: Don't lie to me, save your breath, we both know what the score is. "Is that lipstick? Oh no, don't explain." She's the ultimate realist.

Her voice, often called gritty, gets down here, hits rock bottom. There's nowhere further to go. Her voice is like paint remover or sandpaper stripping the walls. I want to find words to describe her voice, but it's a hopeless proposition, especially with this song, because the whole point of it is: Don't explain. It's the national anthem of anti-hermeneutics, the theme song to Susan Sontag's "Against Interpretation." Washington is trying to communicate to her man about the exhaustion of communication.

In some of these late recordings she approaches the art song tradition. Here, in "Don't Explain," despite the lush Ernie Wilkins arrangement conducted by Quincy Jones, she moves toward a stillness, a hush, and starts deconstructing the ballad lyrics, clawing them apart and looking inside. She reminds me of Edith Piaf, the way she enacts a song theatrically, as it were, as much as sings it. She's been around the block, she has all the street cred you could ever want. And now she's distilling it to bitter wisdom.

On the other hand, there's another way of interpreting that "Hush now, don't explain." "Hush" is what you tell a baby when you're trying to soothe it. So it's possible to read in her voice a maternal quality: she knows her man is still just essentially a big boy and can't help himself. The complexity of her response, simultaneously bitter and maternal, is what makes it so devastating.

It borders on heretical to say that I prefer Dinah's version of "Don't Explain" to Billie Holiday's, but there it is. Don't get me wrong, I appreciate that Billie is the greater artist. The history of jazz runs through Lady Day's voice. All through my teens, twenties, thirties, and forties I listened constantly to Billie Holiday's records, to the point where I knew every note, every phrase, not only hers but the great jazz musicians she played with, like Lester Young and Teddy Wilson. I listened to her so often that I could anticipate each time she sang behind the beat or slid just under the note, and now I can't hear these records afresh anymore, I know them too well by heart. Then I started listening to Dinah. She came a little after Billie. She swung, she was definitely a jazz singer, she played with some great musicians (Clifford Brown, Ben Webster), but there wasn't the same seamless conversation between her and her sidemen as there'd been between Billie and Lester. Whether Dinah sang with a jazz combo, a string accompaniment, or a big band didn't matter: she was always alone.

Billie and Dinah both sounded like the Voice of Experience, but each came out of experience at different places. Billie sounded resigned yet bemused, as though she didn't believe in love anymore but there was still the possibility of hooking up for old times' sake.

She had that detached quality, whether it came from superior intelligence or booze and drugs, maybe both, a liquid sound, like floating on lily pads. Dinah sounded as though experience had made her angry. There was gravel in her growl. As she aged, the voice didn't deteriorate, it just got meaner.

I know I should revere Ella Fitzgerald, her technique is flawless, but she always sounds so clear and cheerful, I can't hear blues in her voice. I'm impressed by her but not in love—my fault, I realize. Sarah Vaughan, especially the young Sarah, "Sassy," is irresistible, the perfect halfway point between Ella and Dinah. But late Sarah sounds tired and mannered to me. Speaking of mannered, for too long I resisted Nina Simone, thinking she dragged out her phrases to an extremity of self-indulgence, often forgetting to swing—though lately I'm much taken with her full-throated, idiosyncratic musicality. She too is in the art song tradition. As for Etta James, she's like a kid sister next to these divas: she hollers, appealingly and well, but it's a little one-note, limited.

Back to Dinah. She was born Ruth Lee Jones, and grew up in the gospel church world, where she acquired vocal intensity. She went from jazz and salty blues to rhythm and blues to pop standards, even country and western, never compromising her passionate delivery, always sounding just like Dinah. According to Nadine Cohodas's biography, *Queen: The Life and Music of Dinah Washington*, she lived a fast life, rapaciously pouncing on those she erotically fancied. Hearing her love songs one gets the impression she did not confuse pleasure-taking with sentimentality. No candles and roses, just cut to the chase. But she was married eight times, which means she couldn't have been so hard-bitten, she must have believed in the romantic dream at moments, or maybe it was that maternal side of her that itched to take care of someone. Her last husband was the football player Dick "Night Train" Lane, who woke to find her next to him, having died in her sleep at the too-young age of thirty-nine from an accidental overdose of pills and alcohol. Her dates are 1924–1963.

Resisting Thinking About Mr. T——

IMMEDIATELY AFTER THE ELECTION of D—— T——, I fell into a funk. I read for a minimum of six hours a day, largely to escape the nightmarish reality of his victory, but also to embrace an activity I knew he rarely if ever engages in, and I also found myself watching more than my usual quota of old movies. Was I depressed? A while back, there was debate in psychotherapeutic circles about whether there should be a distinction drawn between clinical depression and merited sadness, such as the grief experienced when a loved one dies. I realized that technically no one had died, but this turnabout from Obama to Mr. T—— felt like the repudiation of all my values, and the demise of that vaguely optimistic belief (as Martin Luther King Jr. put it) that the arc of history bends toward justice. I was inconsolable.

I soon discovered that everyone in my acquaintance, even every stranger I encountered in the grocery store, thought exactly as I did. We were all mouthing the same lines, repeating the same astonishment at the mendacities, offensive cabinet nominations, and stupefying actions emanating from the White House. Never had my tribe, my cohort, my fellow East Coast elitists and liberal intellectuals been so united, so much on the same page. This should have heartened me, but as the same ideas, the same informational nuggets and argu-ments I had stored up kept boomeranging back at me, I realized it would be almost impossible for me to say anything original about Mr. T——. It is not a happy situation for any writer to discover there is virtually nothing he can declare on a subject of public concern that has not already been said. He can rely on style, of course, but there is only so much style can be expected to do to rescue assertions from the stale or self-evident.

Furthermore, to be honest, I already questioned the notion that the writer has a social obligation to "speak truth to power," or must be "committed" or *engagé*, as the French say. I knew full well the trap of writing crude agitprop poems, or of espousing the kind of misguided support for dubious regimes that even writers as brilliant as Jean-Paul Sartre and Gabriel García Márquez had fallen into, based on their conviction of the necessity to follow a consistent political line. Nor do I think that my name carries enough weight to sway anyone to my beliefs if I were to bother writing editorials and pamphlets. Put another way, I have always shirked the mantle of "public intellectual," and with it the self-confidence and pontif-icating smugness that the term implies. Instead, I have thrown in my lot with the personal essay, which traffics in skepticism, self-mock-ery, and doubt, and is loath to propound anything that is not backed up by individual experience.

My own experience was leading me to resist thinking about Mr. T——: he was like a large sullen child making a great deal of noise, and the louder he got, the more I was repelled by his bluster. He was a black hole in space whose negative magnetism had to be resisted for sanity's sake. As I was withdrawing from his rancid showman-ship, my wife became obsessed with the damage he was causing or threatening to cause: she would read every article pertaining to him in the newspaper, and keep MSNBC or CNN on all day long in the background. Every morning and afternoon Cheryl would engage me in conversations about the latest affront, and I would try to extract myself from these dialogues, which would only reiterate, it seemed to me, what we already knew. In retrospect, her fixation was entirely reasonable, she was trying to digest the indigestible. Nevertheless, I told her (in the spirit of waning patriarchal authority) that she should put herself on a diet of one hour a day brooding about Mr. T——, and no more. She thanked me for this suggestion, though was unable to comply; I myself was unable to follow it, on bad days going over and over the litany of his misdeeds. Meanwhile, my wife clung obstinately to the hope of impeachment, which I regarded as an utter fantasy, given the Republicans' control of both houses of Congress. Even hearing the word *impeachment* disturbed me, as the enervating sound of false hope.

I had stopped watching any TV news the day after the election, restricting myself to reading one newspaper daily to stay abreast of the latest indignities, which I felt civically obligated to ingest. Slowly, I gathered up the courage to watch the local TV news, and to accept seeing his detestable visage from time to time, as an unavoidable fact of contemporary life. Just the other day, I watched a part of his press conference, in which he castigated the media yet again and boasted that he had accomplished more in the first twenty-five days of his term than any U.S. president in history. It was not enough to have bent the truth: he had to pit himself against Washington, Jefferson, Lincoln, Teddy Roosevelt, FDR, Lyndon Johnson, even his hero Reagan, and claim he had outdone them all.

I realized at that moment that there was something very specific about my distaste for the man. His boastfulness made me uneasy, as I could too easily identify with it. I come from a long line of boasters: my father, who otherwise insisted (boasted?) that he was a failure, could not forego bringing up the Latin tests he'd aced in high school; my brother, a radio personality, would maneuver any subject to some form of attestation about his celebrity; and I have struggled unsuccessfully all my life to keep from burping up yet another claim of accomplishment. How many times have I failed to suppress a boast! This man, wallowing in stupidity, keeps crowing about his high ratings and popularity, as though those alone were sufficient to guide the nation. In his naked need for self-approval, I see myself. He is the Mr. Hyde to my Dr. Jekyll. He is already inside me. Can you blame me for trying to eject him from my consciousness by resisting any further efforts to think about him?

Eros in the Classroom

WHEN I AM TEACHING and it is going well, I sometimes have the sense that the pedagogic transaction is occurring not just verbally but through undercurrents that are partly erotic in nature. I feel a tenderness, a longing, or an attraction for students that is similar to someone in love. And I like to imagine that they may feel a comparable warmth towards me.

We live in a time of such heightened sensitivity to sexual harassment that a professor will think twice before telling a student he likes her dress. To admit, as I am doing now, that one sometimes has sexual fantasies about one's students seems risky, tantamount to breaking a taboo, or at the very least icky. But how could it be otherwise, given human nature? I teach in a graduate MFA creative writing program that typically draws many more women than men, and these women, in their twenties, thirties, and forties, are so ardent, so vital, and at such a peak of beauty that entering a classroom can make my head swim. Over the years I've had mild crushes on any number of students: I say "mild" because it never reached the level of obsession, and often years later I couldn't even recall their names, so how deep a crush can it have been?

Let me clarify: I have never dated, much less slept with, a student. I don't expect credit for that: it is simply, as I see it, part of any educator's professional code. When I began teaching, dalliances between professors and their students were common, and often successful marriages came out of them. Still, there seemed an ugly power imbalance about hitting on one's students (though it was not always clear who had the upper hand, the infatuated professor or the experimenting student). In any case, the point, it seems to me, is not to act on those feelings of attraction but to acknowledge and observe them, as they course through my body and around the classroom.

To what extent does it happen the other way? I have no way of knowing whether students speculate sexually about me. I assume it happened more when I was younger. I can remember one time when a very beautiful, married Puerto Rican student made her desire known to me, and I had to let her down gently by treating it as a case of transference: it wasn't "me" she was in love with but some father-figure lover she had projected onto me. In his seminal paper "Observations on Transference-Love," Freud makes a wry qualifying statement: that the analyst must not confuse the structural situation of the patient falling in love with him "with the charms of his own person." This is the tack I have always taken: not that it's happened so often. Usually, women students express no more than a fondness for me. Still, when it happens I have deflected it by acting as if the crush were unreal. I almost said I have *pretended* it was unreal, because deep down I do believe it has some reality. To some extent, all falling in love can be seen as partly unreal by virtue of its distorting element of idealization. But who am I to say that it is also *not* real? If it has been triggered partly by a student's physical attraction to the particular qualities of the professor, which I might happen to possess, if I am her *type*, or vice versa, if she is my type, then—alongside the familial, father-daughter transference—how is it different from any other instance of falling in love? Unless we are prepared to say that all falling in love is bogus, we must be prepared to take seriously the reality of such feelings.

Then, too, there is something falsely modest in the teacher saying: It isn't *me* she fancies, that's only a by-product of the pedagogic situation. If nothing else, this disavowal constitutes a denial of one's allure, which is cowardly, as in any case of the inability to return unrequited love. Why not be honest and admit one has attractive potential? The danger, for the analyst, is in believing he or she possesses some sort of charisma. Nothing could be more vain, grandiose, or ruinous to the psychoanalytic dynamic than for the analyst to assume he or she is charismatic. Can we really believe, though, that Freud himself never made that assumption, when patients came to him from far and wide? In MFA writing programs, such as the one where I teach, there are star writer-professors who attract students from all over, either by the prestige of their works or the renown that has grown around their person. I would wager that all popular teachers harbor fantasies of possessing charisma, however unconsciously, and it buoys them when they stride into the classroom to face a bunch of (conceivably indifferent) strangers. I have often approached a new classroom or an audience at one of my readings and found myself unleashing a stream of excited energy, or improvising jokes, with the intention of winning them over. To the extent that it worked, ought I to credit this as proof that I possess a shred of performance charisma, or ascribe it to the polite respect paid an elderly professional? Who can say? The point is that it is a seduction.

In her astute book about transference, *Death and Fallibility in the Psychoanalytic Encounter*, Ellen Pinsky notes that the analyst acts as a "tease" eliciting erotic feelings in the analysand, then backs away into an abstinent, neutral stance. "The analyst, as transference magnet, in effect courts the patient's passion." A very tricky game, it would seem. But at least there is a good deal of theory in the field about the pitfalls and advantages of this transference/countertransference method. What about teachers of creative writing? Are we conscious of the forces we unleash by our seductions? Are we in control of them? I've seen very little written about this topic in educational literature.

To get back to my own on-the-fly observations: I notice that many ex-students, often the prettiest, seek me out for a chat after they have graduated, saying they miss me and want to catch up. I wonder if they had picked up some erotic spark, some partiality on my part by the number of glances I had directed toward them in class, say, and were flattered by that attention and wanted to see if it was still in operation. They give me hugs, pressing their breasts tightly against me, and kiss me on the cheek, all of which I try to take in the spirit of granddaughterly regard. Some of them return because they were able to write freely under my tutelage, and would like to reanimate that sense of inspiration. Then again, it is not always the young ones who return: Some of the strongest attachments have occurred between middle-aged women and myself, the affection issuing from a wry appreciation of life's challenges and survivals.

I had one such student, Amelia, who had been practicing law for years before she decided she wanted to become a writer. She took several classes with me, and we always enjoyed each other's sense of humor. I did not, I think, have a crush on her, but I simply adored her personality. An activist in her community, she never got on a moral high horse with me: she had a practical, down-to-earth sensibility and was in all respects delightful. Last year she died, suddenly, "of natural causes," we were told (I assume a heart attack or seizure). I have been forcibly shaken by that loss. The assumption is that our students will outlive us, and when they don't, the order of the universe seems shaken. The last lines of Theodore Roethke's poem "Elegy for Jane," dedicated to "My student, thrown by a horse," came immediately to mind: "I, with no rights in this matter / Neither father nor lover." Such is the teacher's lot: to acquire tender feelings for students, to relinquish them physically after graduation, to wish them the best, and to watch them from afar flounder, flourish, or perish.

Because death cut short any further conversation between Amelia and me, I am left to wonder at the nature of the strong exchange that took between us. If I choose to root it simplistically in the word *Eros*, it is partly because I'm a Freudian and lack the philosophical or mystical vocabulary to explain these currents of feeling in other ways. I only know that while I am trying in the classroom or in private conference to put into words the most articulate phrase I can summon, as though I were writing aloud, all this verbal matter provides the cover for an intuitive enchantment. Simply put, we read each other. We breathe in each other's presence with a shared recognition of our comic peculiarities and the poignancy of our being alive together in the same moment, alert and sexy and lonely and fragile. This connection may finally account for the grain of truth in that annoying humblebrag, "I've learned as much from my students as they have from me." What we learn is, finally, each other.

Sadness, Irony, and Equilibrium

I AM ALWAYS PUZZLED when I hear people say that they are avoiding a certain book or movie because it promises to make them sad. "I'm not in the mood for a downer," one friend told me. Me, I am always in the mood for sad art. When I was a teenager, I sought out anything that would put me in touch with the gravest, deepest, and most lugubrious chords. Bach's Passions, Robert Bresson's *Diary of a Country Priest*, *King Lear*, Grünewald, these were my pillows. Dostoevsky was my God. Later on, I was drawn to Kenji Mizoguchi's *Ugetsu* and *Sansho the Bailiff*, films that conveyed a tragic sense of life. The deaths of the father and sister in Satyajit Ray's Apu trilogy moved me to tears. Robert Burton's *Anatomy of Melancholy*—the title alone enticed me. I have to ask myself: Why were these dark descents so consoling? And by what mechanism was I conditioned to transform the worst news about the human condition into the most solacing?

Obviously, I see now, if I were to touch bottom in safe surroundings, like an inky movie theater or at home, holding a book in my hands, and more important, if these negative truths were delivered with sublime artistic shape, that would take the curse off them. I remember reading Thomas Hardy's *Jude the Obscure* the first time, and coming to the end, being transported by the sensation of understanding ... what? The harrowing mystery of life? Hardy has often had that effect on me.

Artfully executed sad art still makes me cheerful. I seek it out whenever I can. At the same time, I have had a long-standing love affair with the ironic artists whose counsel is not to take oneself so seriously. I love the playfully self-mocking fictions of Italo Svevo and Machado de Assis, the Italian film comedies of Dino Risi and Alberto Lattuada, Diderot's *Jacques the Fatalist*, Max Beerbohm's mischievous essays. They form a necessary counterweight to the gravity of the tragedians. Paradoxically, the ironists may have a darker, more sardonic vision of life than the tragedians, because they deny audiences the release, the catharsis of sorrow. Their sole reassurance in giving out the worst news is that one can only laugh.

It was a sign of growing older, I suppose, when I took on Michel de Montaigne as my new master. The extreme intensities I craved as an adolescent suddenly seemed excessive: when I tried to reread Dostoevsky, it all sounded overly hysterical. Why must Raskolnikov and Nastasya Filippovna carry on so? I could still enjoy the Underground Man because he trafficked in bitter ironies, but even he sounded shrill. Montaigne, whose advocacy of equilibrium struck me, when I read him for the first time in college, as self-satisfied, inane, lacking an edge, now affected me as the summit of wisdom. I embraced his sense of balance, proportion, and self-acceptance. "The greatest sin is to despise one's being," wrote Montaigne. Self-hatred suddenly seemed a form of vanity: Who are you to think you're so despicable? Get a grip. The adolescent me was impatient to have life's outcomes resolved: Is life going to be triumphant or catastrophic? If the latter, should I commit suicide? Middle age conditions you to accept that nothing is going to be resolved, nothing is certain, and that somehow is all right. So I have sought a personal aesthetic that will allow for sadness, comic irony, and equilibrium.

One thing has never changed: I've always been a fan of the blues. I have only to listen to a Bessie Smith or John Lee Hooker record to feel life is all right. What Ralph Ellison wrote about it can't be bettered: "The blues is an impulse to keep the painful details and episodes of a brutal experience alive in one's aching consciousness, to finger its jagged grain, and to transcend it, not by the consolation of philosophy but by squeezing from it a near-tragic, near-comic lyricism." In short, the blues offers up agony (it hurts so bad), worldly self-mockery (because you should have known better, you fool), and equilibrium (the sun's gonna shine on my back door someday) simultaneously, in economical, lyrical form. It is the perfect three-in-one vitamin pill.

Celebrity Profiles

I'M NOT VERY FOND of celebrity profiles. We read about movie stars, say, with the hope of catching glimpses of some secret humanity or oddity behind their projected allure, but invariably the results are disappointing. The celebrity has by now mastered the technique of hiding in an interview. We learn only how ordinary they are, just like you and me: hardworking professionals, insecure in middle school, grateful to a teacher, and (this is the promo part I hate most) how much the character they played in their newest film or play is and is not like them. I went through a phase of being fascinated with Claire Danes, then I read a long profile of her in *The New Yorker* and she seemed quite boring, or maybe it was just the way the story was written. In any case, I no longer read any show-business profiles; it saves a lot of time for worthier activities, like watching baseball.

Perhaps one reason for my disenchantment with the form is that years ago, when I would take occasional freelance journalism assignments, I was called upon now and then to interview a celebrity. *Esquire* ran a feature called "Women We Love," and the editors asked me to interview Catherine Deneuve for it. She was going to be in New York promoting her latest picture. She spoke perfect English, so I would not need a translator. When I told a poet friend who was besotted with La Deneuve, his ultimate erotic fantasy, that I was going to interview her, he was beside himself. Although I myself didn't obsess about her, finding her a trifle formal and self-composed, I happily acknowledged that she was a great actress and a great beauty.

My first sighting of her occurred in the Algonquin Hotel, as she strode across the lobby, her breasts jutting forward like a figurehead on a man-of-war. She was every bit as comely in person as on-screen, but she had the chilly, untouchable aura of a professional business-woman, the CEO of Deneuve Limited. We journalists, about seven of us, were taken to a large empty ballroom where we would be given half an hour apiece to interview her—a timetable that put one unfortunately in mind of her brothel role in *Belle de Jour*. Though her haughty, resentful air while submitting to these sessions was understandable, and I pitied her for having to submit to the ordeal, nevertheless we had all been enlisted to promote *her* on this side of the Atlantic. Maybe she had no interest in being further promoted but had undertaken the round of interviews solely at the studio's request. The actress was accompanied by a crew consisting of her hairdresser, her makeup artist, and her personal assistant, and every time an interview ended, she would repair with relief to her entourage. I was struck by how much warmer she was with these familiars than with us, the American journalists. At one point I eavesdropped and heard them enthusiastically plotting with her to go shopping on the Lower East Side when these tiresome inter-views were done.

I was the next-to-last interviewer scheduled, and expected her to be drooping with fatigue. She was, but I had not prepared for the perfect indifference she showed me as a fellow human being, the utter nullity that I apparently represented to her. I could have been a disembodied voice whose questions she was answering in an isolated sound studio. Not that I blamed her: if anything, I was intrigued by my reduced status to Invisible Man. But I took it as a challenge to become real to her, if only momentarily. The way I did it was not to ask her personal questions but only to inquire about her work with various master filmmakers such as Luis Buñuel, François Truffaut, Jacques Demy, Robert Aldrich, and André Téchiné. She became excited talking about these auteurs and their techniques, and revealed herself to be an extremely informed film buff. In our shared love of cinema we may even have established a flickering human connection. I would like to think she began taking me in as someone worth talking to, there may have even been a little eye contact, but I could be exaggerating that in my faulty memory of the scene.

The piece ran as a Q and A, and was no better or worse than it had to be.

The next celebrity profile assignment I received, this time from *Interview*, was to write about Gong Li, the ravishing Chinese actress who starred in many of Zhang Yimou's films. In 1990 I was sent on a junket to mainland China, to the set of *Raise the Red Lantern*, to watch parts of that period film being shot. All the scenes that I saw being shot featured Gong Li, who was playing the role of a newly arrived concubine tormented by her predecessor rivals because of the master's preference for her. Given the fragmented process of filmmaking and the language barrier, I had only the dimmest understanding of the action, and could barely judge the quality of the acting, but I noted the changing shades in the star's facial expressions.

At the time, Gong Li was being called the most beautiful woman in film. She was long rumored to have had an affair with the married director Zhang Yimou, with scandalous consequences, though what

I did not know was that she was also soon to trade him in for a fabulously wealthy Chinese businessman. All this was grist for the mill at *Interview*, the gossipy celebrity tabloid started by Andy Warhol, and in return for my two-week holiday in China, I was expected to engage in a question and answer session with the screen goddess and package some of the dirt for *Interview*'s readers.

The interview took place one afternoon in Gong Li's hotel room, during a break in shooting. She showed up wearing jeans and white ankle socks, looking like a bobby-soxer or a typical twentysomething on her way to the mall. Since she pretended to speak not a word of English, our Hong Kong translator, Norman, acted as a go-between. I would ask a question, Norman would translate, and Gong Li would giggle and mumble a few words. I would look at Norman and he would shrug, trying to fluff up her non-reply into something like an answer. This went on for about twenty minutes. No matter what questions I asked, personal or impersonal, she was equally giggly and unresponsive.

On the plane ride home, I realized I had nothing to work with. I would have to fictionalize the entire interview. So I supplied answers that I thought she might plausibly have made, had she been more forthcoming. I channeled my inner Gong Li. My reasoning was that she would probably never see the magazine, and *Interview* ran it, with no one the wiser. To paraphrase Flaubert, "Gong Li, *c'est moi!*"

I could have written an accurate account of what had transpired. The failed interview or non-interview has become a staple, from Gay Talese's classic "Frank Sinatra Has a Cold" on down to the present. But there are only so many times you can pull off that slippery approach. Ultimately, editors and readers expect you to deliver the goods.

A few years later, I was sent by *The New York Times* to do a story on Christine Lahti, who was starring in a revival of the Wendy Wasserstein play *The Heidi Chronicles*. A fan of Lahti's, I found her intelligent, engaging, and serious in person. The problem was that I disliked the play, which seemed to me pandering to the zeitgeist, and I had to disguise that prejudice in the interview so that Lahti would not pick up on it while she earnestly explained why this particular role was so meaningful to her.

My final experience along these lines was being asked to do a full celebrity profile of Daryl Hannah. I imagined myself hanging around the actress (who had so vividly played a mermaid) for days, watching her going shopping or working the room at a party or speaking to her agent or painting her toenails, and declined the offer. Suppose she turned out to be vacant, like many movie actors: I would feel a heel exposing her vacuity in print. (Actually, I've heard since she is quite intelligent: my mistake.) Though I've regretted my "principled" refusal to do the story on Hannah, the point is that it was too late, I had already come to the conclusion that I was just no good at writing celebrity profiles. Maybe my ego was getting in the way of flattering someone else, but I think it had more to do with the apprehension that I couldn't tell the whole truth about the celebrity, and writing is not fun for me if I have to pull punches. Just as when writing a catalog essay for an art gallery you can never be honest and say the artist's work is uneven, so the celebrity profile is an inherently compromised form.

Joseph Mitchell was expert at writing profiles of noncelebrities: his sympathy for the subjects he chose seemed ensured by their lack of renown. They were just ordinary folks going about their trades or reminiscing. And what a splendid prose stylist he was! I would be tempted to propose him as a model for me to emulate, were it not for a few qualms. It is not simply that everyone's monologues ended up sounding like Mitchell, or that suspicions have been raised after his death that he fictionalized some accounts. More concerning, to me, is the universally benevolent, accepting tone of these profiles: he took everyone he interviewed at their word, which means he failed to consider the rationalizations and outright lies, unconscious or otherwise, to which earthlings fall prey. The most blatant case was Joe Gould, whose self-mythologizing account of writing a great tome Mitchell swallowed hook, line, and sinker. When he finally corrected it years later, in *Joe Gould's Secret*, he seemed stunned by the discovery that his subjects were not necessarily to be trusted, so much so that he never wrote a profile again. Myself, I'm too interested in people's flaws, mistakes, potential for hurting others, the gap between their self-presentation and inner reality, their self-delusions; and such opening-a-can-of-worms curiosities are not recommended for a long and healthy career in the composition of celebrity profiles.

Post No Bills

PLEASE POST NO BILLS I see stenciled in white against a green metal gate in Chelsea. The "please" is a tipoff that the owner lacks authority to enforce his request. And in fact, next to these words and all along the adjoining wall enclosing an empty lot are dozens of posters, some repeated four times like postage stamps. Not surprising that these displayers would want to increase their chances: gashed, defaced, papered over (often before the week is out), city wall posters have a fleeting existence. The aesthetic of partially torn posters, the top image penetrating those beneath like a lap dissolve, has so often been exploited by photographers (Aaron Siskind, Harry Callahan, Walker Evans) and collagists and painters (Kurt Schwitters, Antoni Tàpies) that it's become shorthand for the archaeological layering of disposable, fragmented modern life.

For all its fragility, there is something raffishly outlaw about the medium. One is never sure whether the posters have the right to inhabit their wall or are squatters. Wall poster plasterers operate after dark. Their fly-by-night, legally marginal status is characteristic of the contested nature of public space in the metropolis. Is it all right to sit in the corporate plaza on the concrete lip of a tree pot? The pedestrian gets used to the idea of perching transitionally, like a pigeon, ready to be shooed off.

In sixteenth-century France, the explosion of printing prompted

François I to issue a ban on wall placards. He wanted to control the information that got to the townspeople, but for all his royal power, he did not succeed. Parisians still regard putting up wall posters as their civic right. *Défense d'afficher* has a more somber, bureaucratic sound to it than "Post No Bills," and is resisted accordingly, even when the poster is only a product ad. In New York, what tends to be advertised are not consumer goods but entertainments. Pop concerts, dance troupes, off-Broadway plays, movies of a marginal nature (horror, soft-core indie "sleepers," foreign art films). Never blockbusters: those blessed with real advertising budgets would not stoop to such a low-rent medium.

In the midst of eye-catchers for passing spectacles, one occasionally encounters a political broadside. I remember those put out by a group called the Revolutionary Communist Party, using a one-page newspaper format with screaming headlines that culminated in exclamation points, and below the headlines, column after column of small type. They were obviously modeled on the Chinese Cultural Revolution, but whereas in Beijing a single wall poster might have signaled serious shifts in governmental policy, here they manifested the isolation of those radical Left groups that splintered after the end of the Vietnam War. Their black-and-white fury was like a soot-specked snowball hurled against the wall: a desperate attempt to hold on firmly to a crystalline-pure ideology. There was something touching about the futile effort of these broadsides to persuade, not least because of their old-fashioned belief in the power of words. Their look was so unaesthetic as to exert a perverse appeal: perhaps the most subversive thing about them was their disdain for the nowness of slick graphic design. Paragraph was crammed atop paragraph, in an effort to squeeze a complex political education onto a single page. On a cold winter night, a stroller would risk frostbite by accepting the challenge of reading through such a poster.

Even on a warm night, it was hard to imagine anyone standing before one of these broadsides for the half hour it would take to read every word, not only because the language was so shrill and repetitious but because the typeface became tiny and blurred, as though a speaker, expecting to be misunderstood, had dropped his voice to a mumble. The author of these wall newspapers would seem to have been only partly trying to communicate with the public in earnest. By setting up a labyrinthine course of dense columns which only the most dedicated could follow, was not the Party hoping to ensnare the proverbial one-in-a-thousand, via this spiritual test to find the deserving acolyte? Or was it a matter of anticipating rejection and demonstrating in advance an indifference to popular reaction—speaking directly to the future victors of History, the working class that would emerge triumphant someday and applaud the proper line having been taken?

ONLY GENUINE COMMUNISTS WILL TELL YOU THE TRUTH AND NOT LIE TO YOU! Since so many of these broadsides unmasked a conspiracy (the murder of kickboxer Bruce Lee, the persecution of Brother Bob Avakian, the sinister CIA plot behind the Korean jetliner crash, the collusion of the Rockefellers and the British royals in the drug trade), it was tempting to see these crammed, confusing layouts as the visual analogue of paranoia. The paranoid's discourse often suffers from logorrhea, a kind of nonstop talking to ward off evil signals jamming the mental airwaves, like those madmen who picket the television studios with leaflets about how the networks have stolen their life stories and turned them into popular sitcoms and police procedurals.

It is possible that the Revolutionary Communist Party wall posters are addressed to people precisely of my ilk—wishy-washy liberals—and their headlines may be deliberately intended to irritate us by crossing the line of acceptable caution. Is the motive to push someone like me into radical action, or more likely, to provoke me into showing my true colors as a reactionary?

I will give an example of a headline I saw on one of those wall posters which, so to speak, separates the radicals from the liberals: GENUINE COMMUNISTS ARE THE ONLY ONES QUALIFIED TO LEAD THE STRUGGLE AGAINST ANTI-SEMITISM! From a strictly Leninist perspective, this might make logical sense; however, as a Jew I am so revolted by the suggestion that Jews may not defend themselves against anti-Semitic attacks but must wait for their Communist allies to show them the way that I begin to sputter with rage. At the bottom of this broadside another headline read: FIGHT ANTI-JEWISH ATTACKS BY ORGANIZING THE WORKING CLASS TO TAKE STATE POWER WORLDWIDE! This suggestion rather amused me: It would seem on the face of it a monumentally difficult approach as well as an indirect one, but perhaps not. I am skeptical that the worldwide triumph of the proletariat would necessarily put an end to anti-Semitism. Which would be harder, globally speaking, getting rid of anti-Semitism or organizing the working class to take power? Both are beyond my capacities. I was always taken aback in my youth when I met a radical who would tell me to "organize," inserting the word into conversation with fetishistic confidence. I would never presume to go to the working class and organize "it." When I reencounter such terminology on a wall poster, I feel both nostalgia and embarrassment: the former, as if running into a class-

mate from my youth; the latter, as though faced with an uncle talking
too loudly and inappropriately in front of strangers.

Here is another headline that caught my eye: WE DEMAND 4.1
TRILLION DOLLARS FOR BLACKS AS REPARATIONS FROM U.S.
GOVERNMENT! Sure, why not? I am sympathetic to the scars of
racism, and would like to see justice done, but I wonder how this
curious figure with its decimal point was arrived at. Is the one-tenth
of a trillion supposed to make it sound more scientific? And what
are the chances of successfully rallying masses of Americans around
such a demand? None: the author of the broadside is merely being
provocative. Perhaps it was another case of that strategic ploy I would
hear in the old days, when I hung around revolutionaries: make
seemingly liberal-democratic demands which, proving impossible
to enact, would bring down the system. Wall posters such as these
are a kind of science fiction involving time travel to a utopian or
dystopian future.

Trapped in a Domestic Universe

I LIVE IN a yin-dominated household with a wife, a daughter, and two female cats. In an attempt to provide me with male companionship, we recently got a third cat, a big white Himalayan brute, who indeed seems attached to me, though his motivation may just be opportunism, since I'm the one who feeds him. In any case, I am outnumbered. As the sole male, I am frequently regarded as an alien from another planet, suspected of being clueless. They will issue orders twice, fearing I won't grasp them the first time. They are always fussing over me, straightening my tie or collar, scratching a little toothpaste off my beard. I realize these attentions may indicate they are fond of me, but I feel like their Ken doll. Or their Godzilla. They may yell and scream all day long, but if I raise my voice once, they quiver in alarm: I become in their eyes the archetypally violent male, someone who must immediately seek anger management. At other times they show me unwarranted respect, as though I were some Wise Man. I keep trying to separate how much their responses are geared to me, individually, and how much to their stereotypical notions of men.

Their main charge against me is that I am indifferent to domestic matters, which is largely though not wholly true. When I pipe in with opinions on such matters I am quickly shushed, and told I Just Don't Get It. So I retreat, wounded (if secretly relieved), to my book. When, as often happens, I come home to find the television turned on to a cooking or home repair show, I go upstairs where there is fortunately another TV, and watch sports or an old movie on TCM. Eventually I wander down to participate dutifully in family life, only to intrude upon some mother-daughter squabble, about which I am told to hold my tongue.

It goes without saying (though perhaps I should say it, for safety's sake) that I love my wife and daughter deeply, and my life would be barren and lonely without them. Still, they accuse me of saving my most animated self for my friends, while tuning them out as comparatively duller conversation partners. I try to explain that I see my friends on the average of ninety minutes tops, so it's easy to stay engaged at a high conversational level, whereas I am with them eighteen hours a day, which makes it more difficult to sustain peak engaged performance. It's true: I sometimes resent the amount of mental space domestic matters take up when I would rather be thinking of more intellectually stimulating subjects, such as whatever I am reading at the moment (an excellent biography of Thomas De Quincey by Frances Wilson, and a fine book about existentialism and phenomenology by Sarah Bakewell). But even when I make a good-faith effort to share the housework, volunteering to do the shopping, say, it is generally rebuffed. I am told I don't really know how to select the best fruits and vegetables, or I usually buy the wrong brand of something.

Last week my daughter came up with the bright idea of throwing a Golden Globe Awards party, inviting friends over for chili, salad, drinks, and dessert. I was puzzled: When had anyone in our family cared about the Golden Globes? But it was a pretext to entertain, on a weekend in which our daughter was getting bored with her parents' oldster company, so we decided to honor her request. My wife is always saying she would like to entertain more. We make lists of possible invitees for a dinner party and usually nothing comes of it. I am glad nothing comes of it, because on those occasions when we have had people over, my wife becomes extremely tense in the hours of preparation, convinced that she is running out of time to cook or that the house is not clean enough, and this tension converts to the angry conviction that she has to do everything by herself. Regardless of how much we pitch in, she clings to the belief that it is all falling on her shoulders—perhaps because hers is the commander's vision of what needs to be done and she has a hard time delegating to her troops, who may not do it as well. This time, suffering from a bad cold, she had no choice but to enlist our help. I offered to vacuum, but the job was assigned to our daughter, because "Daddy doesn't vacuum right." I started to object that the last time, I did a *great job* vacuuming, but it was no use, I will never escape the mythological stigma of being an inept vacuumer.

So I was sent out to buy supplies, getting all the food, wine, beer, canola oil, and other necessities. Thinking it might be nice to have some snacks for our guests to munch on before the chili was served, I bought nuts, pretzels, hummus, and veggie chips (this last for a vegetarian friend). My wife exploded when she saw the veggie chips, saying she hated them, they were so old-ladyish and ridiculously expensive, it was one more proof I Just Didn't Get It, and I could bring them to my office at the university for all she cared, but under no circumstances would she ever allow them to be served at one of her parties. I thought it unjust that all my efforts to procure the items on her list were negated by this seemingly harmless purchase, this one petty detail. I have to admit in retrospect it was more or less the way I blew up when she accidentally threw out the Sunday *Times Magazine* before I could do the crossword puzzle, but I preferred to ascribe it to the difference between men (rational, equable) and women (emotional, resentful).

The party came off smoothly, a dozen people showed up, ate all the food, and several stayed glued to the Golden Globes on television while others happily mingled. I noted that my wife and daughter comported themselves throughout as cheerful, charming hosts, showing not a shred of their earlier pessimism or tension. I felt pleased to be attached to them and proud that I, an alien Martian, had contributed to the evening's success, if only as the designated schlepper.

Swimming in the Salmon Stream

ABOUT A WEEK OR TWO AGO I went to the Association of Writers & Writing Programs (AWP) Conference and Bookfair, as I have
been doing every year for quite some time. It's a large gathering, with
upwards of ten thousand in attendance, and it migrates from city
to city. This year's shindig was held in Washington, D.C., at the
Walter E. Washington Convention Center and the adjoining Mar-
riott Marquis hotel. The corridors, escalators, lobbies, and bars were
crammed with seekers—writers and wannabe writers—which was
heartening and dispiriting in equal measure: the former because it's
good to see so many people still attached to books and literary culture, the latter because, like a minnow in a salmon run, you realize
how slim the chances are of getting your own written efforts noticed.

As it happens, I had a new book, which had just come out (*A
Mother's Tale*, published by Ohio State University Press), and was
at the conference partly to "promote" it, if that is the correct word
for spitting into the wind. In the vast, two-football-field-sized bookfair, with hundreds of tables manned by small presses, established
publishers, writing programs, and literary agencies, I sat at the OSU
booth for an hour and signed copies. Like any *schmata* salesman on
the Lower East Side, hoping to drum up business by standing outside

his store, I was cravenly grateful for those who stopped by, chatted, and bought a book.

You would think that after having seen some twenty or more books of mine into print I would by this time be calm and indifferent about the process. Not a chance. I am nervous, anxious, edgy, and will probably stay that way until I get a review in *The New York Times* or some other major media outlet. If none arises, I will brood about the missed opportunities for years. The fact that friends, acquaintances, and relatives have told me they liked the book only makes me tenser: now I think I have a potential winner on my hands, and am frustrated because the university press that kindly published it has the enthusiasm but not the means to market it properly, so it will likely disappear from sight very soon. Yet you must have faith that the right readers will find your book in time, if it's any good. So they tell me, so I tell myself. Oy.

Meanwhile, I spoke on two panels, one on Thursday, one on Friday. The panel discussion is my least favorite form of entertainment: four or five writers get up and speak for ten minutes apiece, then take questions. It is almost impossible for any subject to deepen, to arrive at insight or nuance; the result is a lot of competitive posturing. Moreover, I am never sure whether to interact with the other panelists or the audience. I remember once seeing Harold Brodkey on a PEN panel, putting his head in his hands in a posture of lamentation, like Munch's *The Scream*, as though to block out the mediocrity of the other panel members. How rude! Brodkey was blessed with a massive superiority complex, so his gesture was not entirely surprising, but many times I have thought of duplicating his despairing demonstration, not because I feel superior to my fellow panelists but just because it bores me to participate in such a clunky play.

On the other hand, I like getting up in front of a packed house and improvising remarks. My impatience translates into a mischievous impulse, I find myself accessing absurd free associations. It's a reversal of the solitary act of writing, a repudiation of the alleged lonely soul crying out in the wilderness. I find I trust large anonymous audiences—more, sometimes, than small groups. A therapist once mockingly characterized me as having an "amphitheater personality." Maybe so: I go into a trance and shed my reserved demeanor. For all my misgivings, the two AWP panels, especially the second one, came off well, and the audience left seeming pleased.

In earlier visits to the conference, I used to listen to various panels, but now I attend only the ones I'm on, and the rest of the time meet with friends, colleagues, former students over coffee, a drink, or a meal. These conversational catch-ups are what I like best about AWP conferences: the chance to hear the next chapter in people's lives; their children's recent doings; their projects, illnesses, romances, unsupportive universities; their take on contemporary literary fashions; their students' reluctance to read. There is an avidity with which we tear into each other's lives, and an intense focus that comes partly from knowing we may not see each other for another year or two and partly from our wish to block out the swarm of literary hopefuls around us. One's awareness that there are ten thousand others in the same boat is an insult to one's amour propre.

Most of the young people are there hoping to party, to get laid, or to learn of employment possibilities. We older panelists have not even that excuse. Every year, writers I know tell me that they will never go to another AWP conference again; they are fed up with the mob scene. The implication is that they have matured beyond this cheap need for validation, or for this spurious sense of community—whereas I have not. In truth, I expect to keep coming back as long as they invite me to speak on panels. It is one of the few places where I am treated like a big deal. Strangers come up to me and say that my books have changed their life. I understand they are just being nice and I remain dubious, or I translate their remark into: "Before I encountered *The Art of the Personal Essay* I was financially solvent, but now I am a starving essayist." Meanwhile, their flattery takes my mind off its anxiety about my new book, for a few seconds at least.

The Passing of Robert Silvers

W{\footnotesize HEN SOME NOTABLE PERSON} whom you knew, however slightly, dies, you may find yourself perusing the obituaries and eulogies and disagreeing with this or that characterization. So it was last week when Robert Silvers, the longtime editor of *The New York Review of Books*, passed away. The headline in *The New York Times* called Silvers "self-effacing," and the obituary's writer, William Grimes, after using that term, went on to say that "it was Mr. Silvers who came to embody the *Review*'s mystique, despite, or perhaps because of, his insistence on remaining a behind-the-scenes presence, loath to grant interviews or to make public appearances."

The Bob Silvers I knew was no shrinking violet. He was an extremely proud, self-confident man, completely aware of his stature, achievement, and power, and willing to represent *The New York Review of Books* at any public event. If he was loath to grant interviews, it was probably because he considered them a bore. Everyone remotely attached to the book world knew who he was, admired him, worshipped him, resented him, or feared him. What the obituarist took for self-effacement was in fact a reserved, impersonal manner—the Anglophile side of Silvers, which went with his tailored gray suits, his refined taste for the good things in life, and his insistence that anyone writing for the publication keep a tight rein on their personal effusions.

I first came into contact with the man when I was working for Teachers & Writers Collaborative, a nonprofit agency that sent writers into the schools to renovate the language arts curriculum. Herbert Kohl, an educational reformer (author of *36 Children*), had roped his sometime publisher Silvers into serving on the board of T&W. This was during the sixties, and it was typical of the progressive Silvers that he would support idealistic causes like revolutionizing public schools for inner-city minority youth—albeit at a safe distance. After a short period he stopped attending the board meetings but continued to permit his name to appear on the organization's masthead.

When T&W commissioned me to edit an anthology about the organization on its tenth anniversary, I requested an interview with Silvers about the early days and his involvement in it. The *Review* was then still located in the Fisk Building on West Fifty-Seventh Street, its offices cheek by jowl with law and accounting firms along an endless drab corridor of frosted glass doors. I found Silvers in shirtsleeves and tie, smoking the sweet-smelling dark cigarillos he then fancied, surrounded by precarious piles of books and manuscripts. He dutifully obliged with his time but was at bottom unrevealing, recounting the history of T&W's founding (which I already knew) in an objective, impersonal manner. There were no human-interest anecdotes. I, who prided myself on my ability to establish a warm connection in any one-on-one conversation, had to admit defeat. In the face of this rather opaque personage, I was baffled by getting not even a peek at his inner life.

Meanwhile, I went on to write many books, two of which were

critiqued in the *Review*: the first, *Being with Children*, may have attracted his nostalgic approval because of its emphasis on the work I did with T&W; the second, my novel *The Rug Merchant*, was favorably reviewed by the critic Robert Towers, an acquaintance of mine. Towers also recommended me to Silvers, who was looking for possible fiction reviewers. My dream was to write for *The New York Review of Books*, so naturally I was excited at the prospect. I was sent two novels for a tryout; the novels were wildly different, but I did my best to knit them together in a coherent essay. I thought the results decent, but Silvers took a pass. I later learned that he wanted more plot summary, which I'd been averse to doing. It would seem that the typical *Review* reader preferred not to have to read the book under review but to get enough of a sense of its contents to chat about it.

A few years later, having fallen under the thrall of the Japanese novelist Soseki Natsume, I proposed to Silvers that I write a consideration of the dozen Soseki novels in translation. "We already have our Japanist," he told me coolly. Whatever. It dawned on me that there was a club: the same names kept recurring, and any new contributors could probably be brought in as members only by social introduction. If you did not have the proper entry you would not exist on his radar and would never get in. I tested the waters one more time: Running into Silvers at a library event, I mentioned that I was working on an introduction to the reprint of William Dean Howells's New York novel, *A Hazard of New Fortunes*. "Send it to me," he said. I did, nothing came of it, and soon after, a piece by Arthur Schlesinger Jr. appeared in the *Review*: his introduction to a competing reprint of *A Hazard of New Fortunes*. Of course Silvers chose Schlesinger's over mine (though mine was in fact better). He was in the club; I wasn't.

The sense of being snobbishly excluded cut into my gut. It was that classic literary-world resentment: Why not me? For whatever reason, no matter how much my writing was welcomed elsewhere, I was not to be accepted into this happy band of *Review* arbiters. Was I too rough around the edges? Too Brooklyn, too personal essayish? Too unconnected to the Upper East Side/Upper West Side/London social circles in which Silvers traveled? What made it harder to take was that I could not disparage the rejecting organ because I *loved* reading *The New York Review of Books*. I found it indispensable to my well-being. An early subscriber, remembering the excitement around its first appearance in 1963, I had not missed an issue in decades. Of course some issues were duller than others; but almost always I read the publication cover to cover and came away stimulated or enlightened by something in it. It was and is the standard-bearer for American intellectual life: a unique repository of thoughtful discourse, unrepentantly highbrow, in a culture increasingly given to dumbing down.

Over the last five years, I became a regular contributor to *The New York Review of Books*. How did this turnabout happen? Edwin Frank, the editor of the equally indispensable NYRB Classics, asked me to write an introduction to a novel by the nineteenth-century German novelist Theodor Fontane. Frank sent my introduction to Silvers and he liked it, as he later did my introduction to a collection by the English comic writer Max Beerbohm; both pieces eventually appeared in the *Review*. I proposed to Silvers an appreciation of the American essayist Edward Hoagland, and he accepted the

suggestion. From that point on, every few months he would com-
mission another article. He never discussed them with me in
advance; a package would simply show up in my mailbox which
contained one or more books, with a brief note saying he hoped
I would find them interesting enough to review, and a mention of
the fee. The pay was excellent, and so I accepted them all, not wanting the flow to stop.

The assignments were a catchall of novels, poetry, and essay collections. I still was unsure he really "got" me, knew what my range
of interests were, but clearly he now trusted me. I was in the club.
Contrary to what I had heard, Silvers's editing of my pieces was
extremely light: either he had given up the old battles over each
comma and word choice, or I turned in copy that was more or less
camera-ready. You might say that from my more than fifty years of
reading the *Review*, I had so assimilated the house style that I could
merge my own essayistic manner with its slightly formal, authorita-
tive tone.

I reviewed books by Charles Simic, Joyce Carol Oates, Mischa
Berlinski, Tim Parks, Cathleen Schine, Jane Jacobs, and Eli Gottlieb.
All but Gottlieb were regular contributors to the *Review*, which
made writing about them a tricky proposition. The common jibe
was to call the periodical "The New York Review of Each Other's
Books," and it was true that Silvers loyally assigned reviews of his
contributors' new publications; but I (compromised perhaps by now
being a beneficiary) no longer viewed this as a nepotistic payback.
It may simply have been that he regarded his contributors as worthy
authors, and so why punish them by neglecting their latest work?
Practically speaking, I knew it would not do to savage any of the
regulars' books in my reviews, and in any case, as a fellow writer who

realized what labor it took to compose a book, it wasn't my style to pen vicious pans of anyone. So I drew on a measured, tactful, balanced tone, but when criticism was called for, of course I had to be honest. For the most part Silvers accepted my judgments without demurral, though I could tell it pained him when I wrote a mixed review of Oates's three books. He called me at home a few times to make sure I had gotten some historical facts about the Tawana Brawley case right, without coming clean and admitting that he wished I could have been more positive about two of her three books. It was only when I took the occasion of reviewing a Jane Jacobs biography to question some of her premises that he responded with alarm, saying that I had been too hard on "our Jane," and he was not sure he could run the piece. I asked him for a chance to take another crack at it, which he gave me, and I toned down some of the criticism while buttressing my argument with more evidence. He thanked me for my work, sent me a check, and said he still had some concerns, but the implication was that he would run the piece eventually. With his death, it remains in limbo.

A friend of mine who wrote regularly for the *Review* counseled me that Silvers retained considerable loyalty to the protests of the sixties, and Jacobs, being one of the prime voices of that movement, may have been in his mind a sacred cow. This same friend also thought Silvers was much more engaged by public affairs, political ideas, and burning social issues than by literature, or should I say belles lettres. True enough: essay collections were rarely covered in the *Review*'s pages. He said Silvers would sometimes have long phone conversations with him about the latest public scandal; the editor had a taste for gossip. I kept that in mind when I had lunch with Silvers about a year ago. I had requested this face-to-face repast because it seemed odd that our dealings were taking place entirely through the mail and the internet. Also, I was curious how well we would get along in person.

The *Review*'s office had moved to an old printing house on Hudson Street. I stopped by to gather Silvers and we went to a nearby Japanese restaurant of his choice. He looked healthy and in good form, and our hour-long conversation ranged over history, politics, the arts, and urban affairs. He seemed knowledgeable about everything, and I came away thinking him one of the smartest and most interesting people alive. This time I perceived a warmth, a gusto for life, and a quiet humor underneath the reserve. He still didn't talk much about himself, he obviously didn't like to go in for such intimacies, but when speaking about other subjects he was fully engaged. His interest in the world *was* who he was; consequently, there was no question at all of self-effacement.

I realized I'd probably been getting him wrong forever, thinking him stuffy and snobbish because of my own insecurity. I regretted having missed the chance of having him in my life as a friend—or if not a friend, then a stimulating acquaintance; I had started in too late to get to know this remarkable man. Of course, I realized full well that it had never been up to me: I could not have struck up an acquaintance with him until he gave me the nod, the exquisitely belated signal, that I could be a member of his club.

It was one more instance of a pattern that I have rued all my life: that of meeting famous people socially, such as Allen Ginsberg, Norman Mailer, Elizabeth Hardwick, Susan Sontag, Robert Silvers, or Philip Roth, and not knowing how to follow up in getting to know them better, or rather, not daring to believe that I had been given the nod to proceed further. Better not to presume than to intrude where I might not be wanted.

My memory of Silvers as so mentally sharp and physically vibrant at our recent lunch keeps returning in the wake of his death. I had known he was ill, in and out of the hospital with pneumonia, these last few months, and that the illness had begun around the time when his companion, Grace, the Countess of Dudley, had died in Lausanne, Switzerland. Some of his writers thought he had lost the will to live when she passed away; but I subscribe to the germ theory of illness, and incline to think that no one dies of heartbreak. Moreover, at eighty-seven it must have taxed him physically to keep making those transatlantic flights. I was told he still insisted on editing pieces in the hospital. Even at the gates of death he was loath to name a successor. He had wanted to go out as the working editor in chief of *The New York Review of Books*, and he has had his wish.

On Repeating Oneself

I KNOW A MAN who tells the same conversational bits over and over. He doesn't seem to register to whom he has said what. He is like a jukebox, and if you reference someone or something to which he has formed a ready-made association, he will hit E-6, and out will come the appropriate anecdote. Often these accounts have a boastful quality, conveying as they do some instance in which he was praised for his acumen: his insecure need to assert his worth supersedes any requirement to keep the conversation fresh, but it is all I can do to keep myself from reminding him that he has told me that already.

Let's say the world is divided between those who speak without taking in the identities of their listeners and those who record such information, even the particular circumstances surrounding each verbal exchange. I'd like to think I belong in the latter category—not necessarily out of consideration for the other party. It could be defensive: I watch my listener's face for signs of interest or boredom, to reassure myself that I have his or her attention and it's safe to continue. Yet there are times when I'm uncertain and have to ask the person I'm talking to: Have I told you this already?

In the classroom, I am prone to repeat the same answers to familiar questions. I rationalize that it's permitted because I have an obligation to transmit crucial ideas to those who may be hearing them for the first time (and too bad for those who study with me more than once). When interviewed, I used to try to come up with new responses to often-repeated queries, which only slowed down my delivery. Now I stick with the tried and true. But I wonder if it's simply that my mind has grown threadbare. The older you get, the more you discover you have a limited stock of perceptions, examples, and anecdotes. The mind is a magnet that attracts the same iron filings. We could see this phenomenon as early practice for senility.

To repeat oneself is the fate of the elderly. At the other end of the age spectrum, the young often repeat themselves, but for different reasons. Small children enjoy reiterating nonsense vowels or requesting that the same book be read to them, their growing brains intrinsically bound up with repetition. In adolescence and early adulthood, insecurities abound over whether one has made a good impression, is loved for oneself, or has any power in the world, which can lead to overstressing a point. My daughter, in her twenties, will put in a request to us such as "But you'll see to it that you book that weekend getaway, won't you?" several times in a day. She unreasonably fears she is not being heard, that her needs are not being taken seriously, which results in a tendency to sound bossy. Of course we, being enlightened parents, always pay *scrupulous* attention to every syllable out of her mouth, including her demands, which we try to honor— perhaps not always as quickly as she would like, but still....

My wife has a different repetition pattern. Lying on the couch, taking a break from her busy schedule, she will suddenly utter with a dreamy expression, "I think I'll paint that wall." Her repetitions are addressed to projects she has not yet gotten around to. We've been living in the same house for more than twenty-five years, which she is constantly redecorating or repairing, the house is her artwork,

open-ended and ever subject to improvement. Hence, her proclamations of future intent.

So now back to me (and incidentally, isn't the personal essay a
perfect vehicle for repetitive circling around one's self-image?): I,
being a writer, am always looking for new angles, contrarian ironies,
paradoxes that will undercut stale pieties or received ideas. Even in
daily conversation, I monitor my speech closely, trying to root out
the obvious. In doing so I often stay silent for long stretches rather
than mouth the banal. As a result I am seen by some as stern, forbidding, which I consider completely unfair. I am just waiting for
something original to say. It's true I hate small talk, partly because
I'm not good at it but also because it makes me impatient for some
twist to interrupt the stream of inanities.

Yet I suspect that my writing—most writing—is at least eighty
percent restatement of what has already been written. Or an unconscious plagiarism. We know that art grows from previous art, an
adage even truer of failed art, that vast recycled pile of mediocre
expression lacking any originality. When I first started out as a writer,
I made it a point to read centuries-dead authors and lesser-known
foreign writers. Their voices sounded fresher to me than did my
zeitgeist-soaked contemporaries'; and besides, I reasoned, if I were
to copy them, my appropriations would not be suspected by most
readers, steeped as they are in the current mode. A touch of the
archaic could even masquerade as novel.

Having arrived at a recognizable prose style, I was confronted by
a second problem, known to every creative worker who's been
around for a while: how to keep from repeating and imitating oneself. I set up different technical challenges, tried other genres. But

what I came to understand is that I do imitate myself, gladly. I realize now what my strong suits are and I foreground them, doing what I do best by means that have come to seem to me organic, but that can also be considered a form of self-plagiarism.

I've had the disconcerting experience of reading old diaries and coming upon the same insight repeated every decade or so, with no recognition that I'd already entertained that thought before. I've come upon some college paper of mine written fifty years ago and discovered syntactical turns I still habitually use. Sentence structures can serve as an individual writer's mental fingerprints. If all my books were digitized for purposes of research (an unlikely occurrence, I know), future scholars would undoubtedly find the same syntactical "choices" or reflexes with dismaying regularity.

The classical Chinese painters may have had the right idea: Unlike Western artists, they placed little value on originality, instead striving to replicate brushwork formulae their predecessors had devised for trees and mountains, say, meanwhile allowing their idiosyncrasies to punctuate the landscape as a covert personal signature. It is in the gap between trying to imitate a master and failing that one's inescapable originality emerges.

Natalia Ginzburg, in her marvelous memoir (though she called it a novel) *Family Lexicon*, characterized each of her relatives by the sayings they repeated throughout her childhood—their individualities defined by their redundancies. It was also a favorite trick of nineteenth-century novelists to bestow on each minor character a turn of phrase as a verbal tic. Balzac's habit of assigning to his characters a single obsession, an idée fixe, may seem reductive to readers today, immersed as we are in critical theory that doubts the cohesive self, but it has considerable validity. We might regard each one of us as parrots, cawing the same paltry impressions, boasts, disappointments, and laments. Rather than disdaining the repetitions of others, or feeling secretly ashamed of our own, we should view them with tolerance as our inevitable postlapsarian inheritance. Blame, if you must, Adam and Eve, who, encountering life's every moment with fresh wonder, opted instead for knowledge, which is invariably mounted on precedent, and in biting that apple swallowed along with knowingness the curse of eternal recurrence.

To a Passing Stranger

WALTER BENJAMIN CALLED IT "love at last sight," that phenomenon of passing an attractive stranger in the street, which is so much a part of the flaneur's eroticized yearning in metropolitan life. He was referring to the poem by Charles Baudelaire, "In Passing," which ends with the lines:

Lovely fugitive
Whose glance has brought me back to life!...
Of me you know nothing, I nothing of you—you
whom I might have loved and who knew that too!

It is precisely because passersby know nothing of each other that such encounters retain their romantic purity. Were the passersby to take it further, the perfection bequeathed by anonymity would shatter. Knowledge of the other's quirks, ineptitudes, flaws, bad manners corrodes the ideal, even as it enriches the reality. The poet might have found the lovely fugitive's taste in books conventional, her complaints about her boss irritating, while she would likely discover his tedious artistic egotism. Perhaps it was for the best that the two remained platonic solids intersecting on the sidewalk's plane. There is magic to unsatisfied desire, which allows for an ever-postponed fulfillment in the future. Recall Walt Whitman's poem, "To a

Stranger," treating the same subject of a passerby crush as Baudelaire, but in a different key:

> Passing stranger! you do not know how longingly I look upon you,
> You must be he I was seeking, or she I was seeking, (it comes to
>   me as of a dream,)

He goes on to say:

> You give me the pleasure of your eyes, face, flesh, as we pass, you
>   take of my beard, breast, hands, in return,
> I am not to speak to you, I am to think of you when I sit alone or
>   wake at night alone,
> I am to wait, I do not doubt I am to meet you again,
> I am to see to it that I do not lose you.

I am to wait . . . I am to see to it that I do not lose you. How hopeful of Whitman, especially compared to his fatalistic contemporary Baudelaire, who immediately gave up the object of his desire. On the one hand, the Frenchman even seems to be blaming the woman who has captivated him ("and who knew that too!"), as though she were a heartless coquette; but on the other hand, he is also positing a genuine connection that might have occurred in their exchange of glances, whereas Whitman ascribes no more agency to the stranger than to an abstract dream figure, who visits him at night like a succubus.

Here is something to confess: Your speaker also likes to look at pretty women in the street. And the strange thing is that I find myself doing it more now as I approach the age of being *hors de combat* than when I was younger and might have had occasion to act on the impulse. I passed a beauty in the street the other day. She did not notice me, she was talking on her cell phone. Or perhaps she did take notice of me but immediately ruled me out as of no interest, I being a graybeard and she so young and lithe, with a shapely figure and bold, intriguing eyes. We men are taken to task nowadays for describing with enthusiasm women's body parts—the objectifying male gaze, it's called. I would not dream of reducing a woman to her body parts; I was fully aware that the beauty I passed might have possessed a complex psyche, an admirable spirit, and a nuanced intelligence, which I would have loved to learn more about had I been given the chance, but I was also noting the plain fact that she was lovely, and in any case, how was there time to register more than her face and figure when she disappeared so quickly?

Was she Japanese? Filipina? Hispanic? I couldn't be sure. All I sensed was that she held a foreign allure. Part of me would give a lot to be other than who I am, the child of Russian and German Jews, or, failing that, to be *with* someone from a different culture or background than mine; yet such attraction is now considered dis-reputable—*exoticizing*, as in: projecting a set of caricatured signs based on outward appearance. Still, I ask myself: Why is it a sin to feel excited when a lovely foreign-looking stranger crosses my path? Is it not one of the prerogatives of urban living? The great Iranian filmmaker Abbas Kiarostami said, "One of the reasons I love New York City so much is that on its sidewalks I see so many nation-alities and not that many Americans." If it was good enough for Kiarostami....

I would never stake out a post just to ogle women: the beauties that pierce my heart must occur serendipitously in passing. I never know whether any will appear on any given day, and I must be in locomotion too, on an errand that has nothing to do with them.

As for being attracted to those women from another class or ethnicity, I'm reminded of a passage in Proust, when Marcel, driven in Mme. de Villeparisis's carriage in the country outside Balbec, fantasizes about a pretty girl walking down the road. He feels

> the desire not to let this girl pass without forcing her mind to become aware of my person, without preventing her desires from wandering to someone else, without insinuating myself into her dreams and taking possession of her heart. Meanwhile our carriage had moved on; the pretty girl was already behind us; and as she had—of me— none of those notions which constitute a person in one's mind, her eyes, which had barely seen me, had forgotten me already. Was it because I had caught but a momentary glimpse of her that I had found her so attractive?

He imagines getting to know this milkmaid "as fully as I wished." His fantasy is not that dissimilar from one the narrator in Jack Kerouac's *On the Road* has, of settling down with a Chicana he sees on a bus in Bakersfield, California.

I realize there is something pathetic, possibly insulting and condescending, about these intellectual types who daydream of a simpler life with women of a lower social class. However, both Proust's and Kerouac's protagonists were young men, and had more of an excuse for letting their libidos run away with their imaginations than I. Am I sounding defensive? You bet. It may even strike the reader as indecent that a man my age should still admire younger women, regardless of these efforts to wrap myself in the borrowed literary authority of a Baudelaire, Whitman, Benjamin, Kerouac, or Proust. Though I never act on it, I will nevertheless be seen as a dirty old man just for thinking such thoughts. The trouble is that while the rest of my body deteriorates with leg pains, prostate worries, sunspots on a bald pate presaging melanoma, my eyes have remained as youthful as a teenager's, and I can still espy at twenty paces a pretty passing stranger.

When I *was* a teenager, working as a messenger in the summers, I would gasp at the young Puerto Rican women ascending the subway staircase to their office jobs. Even then, exoticizing. Not that I would have dared shout out a compliment. But a lovely woman I knew told me she had no objection to men accosting her in the street with amorous intent, it was that they were invariably the *wrong* men. Or would you become the wrong man simply and instantaneously by expressing appreciation for a woman's looks? What about the beauty I passed the other day? Would she have given me a chance to buy her coffee if I had been thirty, forty, fifty years younger and had come up with amusing patter? Doubtful.

All I know is that I fell in love with her for a moment or two, then ten minutes later found myself unable to retain her image. She was the most recent addition to that Etch A Sketch I had superimposed and then erased of all the women I've become infatuated with in the street. She would have every right to take offense at my promiscuous gaze were she to suspect its predecessors. Still, it would be nice to think that with any luck we will meet on the other shore. An old saw has it that Muslim martyrs are promised a hundred virgins in Paradise, but all I ask is that, when I die, I might renew the acquaintance of those passing strangers, those sidewalk Venuses who have throughout my life persisted in eluding me.

Skyping Brazil

LAST WEEK I participated in a PhD dissertation defense for a graduate student at the University of São Paulo. This student, Daniel, had looked me up a year before, during his research semester at Columbia, to talk about the great English essayist William Hazlitt, on whom he was writing his dissertation. He was familiar with several things I had written about Hazlitt, and considered me something of an expert on the personal essay. Not to bore you with false humility, I am. Always happy to encounter another Hazlitt enthusiast, I chatted amicably with him, and then he emailed me asking if I would serve on his dissertation committee. I said yes, hoping it would lead to a paid trip to Brazil where I have never been, but he emailed back a few weeks later to report that sadly the university did not have the funds for my airfare. Would I still be willing to serve on his committee? Having semi-committed myself already, in too deep, I said yes, and kept my fingers crossed that his dissertation would be decent.

A copy of that document, which he had translated from Portuguese to English for my benefit, arrived in the mail. It turned out to be stimulating: Daniel had read all the original material and secondary sources, plus a good deal about eighteenth- and nineteenth-century periodical literature, Hazlitt's literary forebears and contemporaries, and the political, religious, and philosophical debates of the time. If it lacked an overall argument, the prose itself was full of ideas and enthusiasms. (This would be the first dissertation on Hazlitt in Brazil.) In short, it was not academically sterile.

Many preliminary emails followed about setting up the Skype exchange. I must admit I am leery about Skype, mistrustful that it can possibly work and that conversationalists can see each other from thousands of miles away. In spite of the fact that I have done it a few times in the past, I am never sure I can get it to work.

As it happened, the morning of the defense I came directly from a tennis lesson and had no time to shower or change out of a grungy, sweaty t-shirt before sitting down to my laptop. I felt bad that these professors would have to be subjected to my recently perspiring, odoriferous body—conceptually, of course, since only my voice and image would be transported. I managed to get Skype to work and saw an empty classroom in Brazil, its window revealing a sunny day with students walking by on campus. Shortly afterward, the chair of the meeting came on-screen. I could see him clearly, big as life. He could hear me fine but could not see me. They sent for a technician, who suggested the problem was on my end: I had failed to turn on the camera. I managed to locate the camera icon, and suddenly I saw myself in a small box at the bottom of the screen, looking like a shrunken head, a homunculus. Now we were in business.

The chair addressed me graciously in English, saying how "honored" they were to have me there, how "distinguished" I was, and so on and so forth, how much they wished they could have afforded to pay for my visit and taken me out to dinner after but perhaps sometime in the future.... I found these flattering remarks completely appropriate. However, I now had to gear up and play the part of the Distinguished Authority, to mouth brilliantly learned remarks, hard to do at any time but even harder when they were seeing me in this grungy t-shirt advertising Florida sharks. Don't ask me how I got it: I think my wife and daughter brought it back for me from vacation. In any case, I was warned that much of the discussion would take place in Portuguese, but they would try to translate after each speaker. Four respondents were to speak about Daniel's dissertation for half an hour, and I was to go first. *Half an hour!* I had expected to make a few impromptu remarks off the top of my head, in the informal manner of defenses I'd attended north of the border, and had by no means prepared a lengthy discourse. After all, I wasn't getting paid for this. . . . It was starting to resemble one of those nightmares where you are thrust onstage to sing a song whose lyrics you have mostly forgotten.

I began by apologizing that I was not, strictly speaking, a trained academic but a belletrist, and thus could not be expected to hew to that rigorous standard. Then I summarized my impressions of Daniel's dissertation, while he sat facing me, taking notes, looking tense and nervous. He is a handsome, engaging young man in his early thirties, with a burning dark-eyed stare and a bushy black beard, rather like the actor Edgar Ramírez who played Carlos the Jackal in the Olivier Assayas–directed biopic, and I began to wonder, as I was talking and looking at him, what circumstances had brought him to this point in his life—his family background, his past history—to this meeting where he had to defend his passionate enthusiasm for the temperamental, combative William Hazlitt. What had possessed him to put all his eggs in this one basket of a little-known (in Brazil) English essayist? Clearly he was the sort of brainy, restless intellectual who spends a lifetime moving from subject to subject: he had already, it turned out, gotten degrees in philosophy and political science, before switching to literary theory.

Daniel responded deferentially to my critique—which was more appreciative than critical, in any case. Then an ex–philosophy professor of his spoke in Portuguese (later translated for me), stressing connections between Hazlitt and the English and Scottish philosophers who had preceded him and were involved in concepts of sympathy and empathy. This was followed by a twenty-minute break for coffee and snacks, during which I showered and put on a jacket and tie. Now I was more formally dressed than the others and felt able to hold my own.

The discussion throughout the day continued on a very high level, and I was in heaven, listening to all this intelligent chatter about the essay as a genre. I was transported back to the world of nineteenth-century English coffeehouses, where you could pick up a copy of *The London Magazine* and read the latest essays by Hazlitt, Charles Lamb, and Leigh Hunt, or a poem by Wordsworth, Coleridge, or Keats. How wonderful that all these Brazilian scholars were so conversant with English literature! I found myself indulging in that old fantasy of academic life as a Community of Scholars, whose only interest is the advancement of knowledge. Suddenly there were no territorial squabbles, no careerist networking or mutual back-scratching, no stabs in the back over tenure. Fortunately I knew nothing about the internal academic politics of the University of São Paulo, and so I could freely admire the worldliness, nobility, good humor, and far-ranging intellect of these Brazilian professors, more so than I might the colleagues at my home university whose pettiness I knew only too well.

Some of the respondents were harder on Daniel, one in particular legitimately questioning his diffuse profusion of topics. He thought that Daniel had wasted too much time defining the essay as a genre, when he would have been better off taking that for granted and concentrating more precisely on Hazlitt's style. His real reservation, it came out, was that Daniel had only recently wandered into literary studies from other disciplines and had not yet mastered the technique of close textual analysis. I could not help identifying with Daniel, as though they had spotted my own lack of scholarly rigor, and becoming protective of him in the summation period. No need to worry: their approval of his dissertation was never in doubt. The day's proceedings ended with a ceremonial reading of the committee's acceptance statement. Everyone clasped Daniel's hand, and he broke out in a relieved smile, his body relaxing for the first time all day. I shut off my Skype function and with reluctance left Brazil. I was back in Brooklyn.

The Enigma of Literary Reward

THERE IS NOTHING MORE BECOMING in an author than modesty. Regardless of what egotistical airs they may put on, most writers, I suspect, have a fairly accurate assessment of their own achievement. Susan Sontag noted regretfully in her diaries that she was not a genius. I could easily say the same about myself. Still, we are dependent to an uncomfortable extent on the world's judgment, perhaps hoping that by some fluke the world will rate us higher than we can rate ourselves. The problem is not that the world so often ignores literary effort (though that is certainly the case) but that to the degree it breaks its silence it tends to distribute the rewards in a mystifyingly erratic manner.

There seems to be no logical pattern discernible in the honors, fellowships, and glowing reviews it bestows or does not bestow on writers who have achieved a level of professionalism. Why should Writer X get so much attention, when the equally accomplished Writer Y gets next to none? Writer Z must try to make sense of the clashing kudos and snubs she has received, the flatteries and cold rejections, when underneath it all lies the suspicion there is no sense to be made.

Of course there are those rare American authors who, once placed in the limelight, manage to stay there: let's say, two dozen in any given era. I can't speak for those anointed ones, those household names, those demigods; my experience is rather in the other camp, with the thousands of midlist writers whom the reading public may be dimly, subliminally aware of—or not. Much teeth-gnashing, cursing, and praying can be heard from this camp. Its occupants have not yet given up the dream of ascending to the Club of Two Dozen via some "breakthrough" book, splashy advertising campaign, or other fata morgana, and what keeps them in a state of constant suspense is that from time to time a bone *is* tossed to them—a flattering review, say, a runner-up designation for a literary award, or, best of all, a university post. If the world were to deny them any recognition, they could at last resign themselves stoically if not cheerfully to their nonentity status. But it is the inconsistent application of applause and indifference that makes one's situation tormenting and drives one into lesser or greater fits of paranoia.

How are we to keep a firm grip on our own sense of worth when the authorities dish out such random responses? How are we to stop obsessing about "them," the reward givers? You have never won a Guggenheim Fellowship and you fume: those cowards, those bozos! Then one day you do win a Guggenheim and think, they are mighty fine fellows, those judges, and are happy for a month before other thoughts settle in: Why, if you are a good enough writer to win a Guggenheim, have you never won a Lannan or Whiting, much less a MacArthur? Those cowards, those bozos. You are admitted to the American Academy of Arts and Sciences but never hear a peep from the American Academy of Arts and Letters. What to make of it? An enigma. You receive fine notices in *The New York Times Book Review* and the Cleveland *Plain Dealer*, but nothing in *The Wall*

Street Journal or *Bookforum.* Why? It is not the negative reviews that rankle but the non-reviews. There is a picture in my mind of some book review editor who holds my latest book in his hands and decides, "Nah, skip it." Some of these people I run into at holiday parties and literary events. How can these traitors look me in the eye? How can they sleep at night, those cowards, those bozos.....

Such is the fruitless, hamster-like mental scratching that greets me when I awake in the morning, or while waiting for the subway train. Just about now I can hear the angry snorts from writers who are still struggling to break into the big leagues: How dare this guy who has gotten a fair amount of recognition, compared to us, whine about not having enough? I sympathize completely with their disgust, but in truth, it is never enough. Imagine the pangs Philip Roth must have felt each time the Nobel Prize in Literature was announced. The world's refusal to honor you in a consistent manner cannot help but be taken personally, and the resulting fever requires extraordinary maturity to contain.

With so much war, poverty, injustice, and environmental degradation afoot, aren't I ashamed to be worrying about my literary status? Yes and no.

Chagrin is an illness. I try to master it. I put myself on an envy-free diet, and limit the number of minutes I will allow myself to brood, after discovering that So-and-so, one of my contemporaries, has just won a major award. As soon as I find myself thinking, "I may not be such a great writer, but he or she is no better than I am," I switch mental currents into another, equally absorbing topic, such as the demise of the Knicks in the playoffs. Or I count my blessings. Regrettably, I have never been very good at counting my blessings. I am much better at counseling sane resignation to my writer friends in the grip of fury at a literary snub. I tell them that even to call it a "snub" is a stretch, as it implies willful neglect when there may be nothing more here than the long odds against public acclaim, or the imbalance between our capacity to generate desires and our inability to satisfy them.

A friend of mine, an excellent writer, is convinced there is a conspiracy excluding him from certain rewards and publications. Surveying the field, he calculates the present advantages of race, religion, gender, generation, genre; the lamentably low aesthetic standards of the current cultural moment; and the charlatans who act as our literary gatekeepers. I consider him, like most of the paranoia-inclined, an optimist. If only it were that simple. If only we could lay the blame on a sinister group of fashion-conscious power brokers (those cowards, those bozos!) who get together every first Monday of the month at, say, the Century Club to determine the season's winners and losers. No, I am a pessimist in such matters: I see nothing but randomness, pure randomness.

Fortunately, the solution to such a painful dilemma is always close by. I am referring to a sense of perspective. We are all soon to be dust and ashes under the aspect of eternity, a comfortingly modest thought. There is nothing, I repeat, in an author more becoming than modesty. I myself am, when all is said and done, exquisitely modest. I recognize my talent is a small one, and it has taken me further than I ever imagined when I started out on the writing path as an adolescent. So I will conclude by expressing my abject gratitude to the Powers That Be for recognizing me to the degree they have seen fit. We will leave it at that.

Remembering Cynthia Macdonald

I FIRST ENCOUNTERED Cynthia Macdonald, the distinguished poet and my future colleague, when we were booked to give a joint reading in some godforsaken venue on remotest Long Island. We decided to take the Long Island Rail Road train together, and by the time we had done the reading and ridden back and forth, we were friends. She, a witty conversationalist and a writer who employed humor, the grotesque, and sardonic self-mockery in her poems, suited me very well. Besides, I've always been drawn to elders (I was in my late thirties at the time, and she in her early sixties), feeling more rapport with my parents' than with my own generation's cultural sensibility.

Cynthia had just become the cofounder, with poet Stanley Plumly, of a new creative writing program in the University of Houston, and was assembling a faculty. She invited me to apply as the program's first prose writer. Before that I had mostly taught children, but I interviewed and was hired for a tenure-track professorship (my first), and will forever be grateful for her confidence in me.

Eager to please, and to embrace this new Southwest metropolis, I gadded about Houston, making acquaintances—to such an extent that one night Cynthia took me aside and complained that I was getting invited to more dinner parties and social events than she was; it therefore behooved me, as having been initially taken under her wing, to share the wealth and the invites.

Cynthia was pretty popular herself, but she intimidated some people with her imperious manner: she could be a bully, especially to underlings. (I once heard her bawling out the kitchen staff at a literary luncheon she had sponsored, because she thought the chicken underdone or overdone, I forget which.) I was not intimidated by her, having grown up with a mother who was similarly theatrical, domineering, and overweight. Cynthia was very fat, if one can still use that word (if not, please substitute corpulent, hefty, avoirdupois-challenged, or any term of your choice); but as is often said about plump women, she had a pretty face. So pretty, in fact, that she looked twenty years younger than the over-sixty she was when I first met her. From her jacket photos, always headshots, you would never have imagined the girth that billowed under her fetching features—the clear, sparkling eyes and smooth unwrinkled skin. She had been an opera singer and was built like those stout Wagnerian divas that used to be permitted at the Met before the new crop were told to go on diets, as younger audiences would no longer accept so burly an embodiment of a young maiden. She still had a lovely dramatic soprano, and I remember once, leaving a party, we sang a duet to each other, "Only make believe I love you." We both revered the Great American Songbook, and there was something piquant about the choice of that particular song from *Show Boat*, which allowed us to camp our quite real, though non-amorous, affection for each other.

Ambitious for the University of Houston creative writing program, she would preside over the writing faculty's once-a-week meetings, alerting us to possible machinations against our staffing, curricular, or budget requests. Our program was nestled in the English Department, and some of the regular English professors resented our lower course loads and the fuss made over us in the press. Whenever an administrative logjam arose, she would immediately go over the heads of the English Department, straight to the dean or the provost. She would, to use an unfortunate figure of speech, throw her weight around, which made the English faculty even more resentful. I sometimes took it upon myself to soothe their feelings by bridging the two factions—playing the regular guy to offset her queenly airs. But I too could be dazzled by her access to the higher reaches of university administration. One time, Cynthia took me along to a meeting with the provost: it was understood that she was to do the talking and I was there to second her. Some rebellious spark got into me, and at the end of the meeting I said that maybe he and I could have a chat sometime, just the two of us. In my overstepping, I rationalized that I thought he could profit by hearing another point of view about the creative writing program. She was understandably furious at me when we left, and chewed me out good and proper.

Over the years, she recruited a stellar group of writer-teachers, which included Donald Barthelme, Edward Hirsch, Richard Howard, Rosellen Brown, Adam Zagajewski, and Ntozake Shange. Alongside her teaching and administrating, Cynthia also produced one poetry collection after another: her poems, often in the voice of invented personae like Elizabeth Barrett Browning's dramatic monologues, allowed her to be playfully performative while slipping personal emotions of confusion, loneliness, and unfulfilled desires into the voice of others.

Over time I came to learn the broad outlines of her life: her difficult childhood in the home of well-off New Yorkers who divorced, her adoration of her successful screenwriter father, her glamorous mother's neglect of her, her discovery of food which led to her being ostracized by her snotty private school classmates as the chubby girl, her winning competitions as an opera singer, her marriage to a Shell Oil executive with whom she had two children and who moved the family around a lot (putting an end to her singing career), their divorce, her immersing herself in a graduate writing program and launching herself as a poet.

She had struggled all her life with a weight problem, finally surrendering to obesity. Her doctors told her she should try to walk as much as possible for exercise; I remember once accompanying her around Bell Park, a square block in Houston, Cynthia walking very slowly, step-by-step, and confessing what a strain the excess weight put on her breathing and heart.

Cynthia was an enthusiastic booster of Houston, especially its institutions of high culture, and would sometimes invite me to that city's opera, symphony orchestra, or ballet. It was a treat to go to the opera with her, because she knew the repertory so well. Something like Puccini's *Turandot*, which I might have rejected on my own as sentimental fluff, acquired a charm when seen through her eyes. For my part, I would invite her to esoteric revival films at the Houston Museum of Fine Arts, which I co-programmed as a hobby. Always game, she was not by any means a film buff, and could not understand my reverence for Roberto Rossellini's *Stromboli*, which she thought ridiculous and Ingrid Bergman's turn to God at the end hilariously improbable. (Interesting, in retrospect, that she could accept the most preposterous plots in opera but scoffed at the first sign of melodrama in a movie.) I, however, was that absurd creature, a cinephile, and one aspect of cinephilia is being able to love slow, ruminating pictures like *Stromboli* and to find in them a profound spirituality.

To my surprise, she embarked on a third career as a psychoanalyst, earning her degree at the Houston-Galveston Psychoanalytic Institute and setting up in private practice, while continuing to teach and run the writing program. She had always been generously supportive to her writing students—well, most of them, anyway—and that maternal concern, compassion, and wisdom must have needed another outlet. Her specialty was handling clients with writer's block.

It seemed she could do anything she put her mind to, though occasionally she spoke wistfully of her desire to write prose, a novel or perhaps a memoir, and would ask me for advice on how to proceed. I was unsure what to tell her: Keep a diary? If and when she was ready, she would do it, simple as that.

After eight years at the University of Houston, I got homesick for New York City and moved back. We stayed in touch, and every few years I would see Cynthia in the city, usually during the summer or Christmas holidays when she would reoccupy her large prewar apartment on the Upper West Side, overlooking the Museum of Natural History. It seemed to me that she got sweeter as she aged. Or maybe it was that I was no longer her junior colleague, so she could engage me warmly as an old friend, without tightening the reins.

Eventually, as happens too often with ex-colleagues who try to maintain a friendship, we drifted out of each other's sight. One day I heard from a mutual friend, Sally, that she had become senile. The onus had fallen on her resourceful daughter, Jennifer, an installation artist, to take care of her mother, and she was obliged in the end to put her in a nursing home uptown. Every few months, Sally and

I would say to each other, "We really should go visit Cynthia," and then do nothing. Was it the thought of how depressing it would be, the chance that she might not even recognize us, or simply a selfish unwillingness to make the effort and "waste" an afternoon? I realize now how wrong I was: we should have gone. By the time I had worked up the will to do so, I learned that she was in a nursing home out west somewhere. According to her *New York Times* obituary, she died at the age of eighty-seven in Logan, Utah. Why Utah, of all places? Well, eighty-seven is a full life, I tell myself, and she had accomplished so much. But still—that such a force of nature as Cynthia Macdonald *could* die was disturbing and incredible in itself.

Movie Dates

A DEDICATED MOVIE BUFF from my teenage years onward, and an assiduous if not pedantic completist forever seeking out obscure backlist items by favorite auteurs, such as that rare screening of George Cukor's *The Model and the Marriage Broker* (Thelma Ritter gives a great performance), I was perfectly willing to go on such hunts by myself, knowing they might strike others as geeky. Did I really need to subject another to uncovering intermittent personal touches in Douglas Sirk's *Captain Lightfoot*? Still, as a bachelor on the loose, wanting to impress women I was dating while closing a cinephile gap, what better way to win someone over than by treating her to a filmic masterwork? It turned out movie dates proved a problematic seduction tool: cinematic and carnal ravishment sometimes were at cross-purposes.

It started in high school when I took Maureen, a lovely senior and in fact the runner-up that year for Miss Venus, to Carl Dreyer's *Passion of Joan of Arc* at MoMA. By the time Maria Falconetti had perished in flames, my own hopes for a romantic conclusion to the evening had been barbecued. She was not in the mood to snuggle.

But it was another experience years later that crystallized in my mind the quandaries of the movie date. I was going out for the first time with a tall, attractive if solemn blond named Susan who was engaged in numerous antiwar causes. I would be taking her to see

Kenji Mizoguchi's *A Story from Chikamatsu* (also known as *The Crucified Lovers*). This 1954 film, which had never been shown before in New York, was being screened in a new print at Dan Talbot's New Yorker Theater, and I could not be more eager, because Mizoguchi was perhaps my favorite filmmaker. As it unfolded on-screen, I was in heaven: the picture's perfectly composed black-and-white images were every bit as magnificent as I had hoped. The tragic tale of a romance between a scroll-maker's wife and his apprentice, and their doomed attempt to escape punishment and death, had that rich sense of inevitability that I so prized in Mizoguchi: his pacing and ability to keep opening up spaces like a Japanese scroll even as he was closing down narrative possibilities for a happy ending had me in thrall. It was possible for me to absorb the film simultaneously on both dramatic and formal levels: to be pulled into the story of the lovers at the same time as registering every deft shift in camera position, apt lighting choice, and judicious cut. When the lights went on, I was almost in tears. Susan seemed thoughtful: over dinner, she said the film was all right, a little dated perhaps, and wondered why I'd been so moved. I couldn't explain it to her, nor did I wish to relinquish my high, even as it doomed me to feeling isolated.

Without realizing it, I had put her through a test—an unfair one. If she and I had been on the same page vis-à-vis Mizoguchi, well then, who knows? Marriage and kids might have followed. I knew her lukewarm response was perfectly reasonable, given her normal citizen's investment in movies. She was a highly moral person pondering the film's ambivalent attitude toward adultery, and I was this delirious aesthete, a collector of rare, almost forgotten cinematic jewels, who had just gotten his dream wish. Having put in thousands of hours studying film in general and Mizoguchi in particular, I was at a loss as to how to explain to her what was so remarkable about his mise-en-scène, his precise directorial choices. There was no second date. Maybe taking someone to a movie titled *The Crucified Lovers* might not have been the best way to initiate a romantic affair.

At the time I did not pursue Susan further because I thought her somber and humorless, which was true; on the other hand, it had been my own solemnity and lack of humor regarding the transcendental masters of cinema that prevented me from connecting with her. This kept happening. Though I think of myself as an ironic, skeptical type, I had completely bought into the expression of transcendent spiritual conviction by those master filmmakers I most admired, such as Mizoguchi, Rossellini, Dreyer, or Robert Bresson. The ending of Bresson's *Pickpocket*, for instance, when the hero, having been imprisoned, is finally able to accept the love of Jeanne, seemed unquestionably beautiful. Bresson's *Les Dames du Bois de Boulogne*, shown in New York for the first time in decades, enthralled me, but I was dismayed when some of the audience tittered at the ending. The audience seemingly had no training in melodrama and snickered at outbreaks of pure feeling. I kept revisiting on my own the Rossellini-Bergman cycle, like the finale of *Journey to Italy*, finding the married couple's unexpected reconciliation tremendously moving, but realizing it would seem arbitrary and unconvincing if one wasn't a card-carrying cinephile on the lookout for miracles.

I had a much happier outcome when I took a woman, Connie, to a press screening of Jean Renoir's *Elena et les hommes* (*Paris Does Strange Things*). Another film that had been out of circulation for decades, rereleased in a gorgeous color print, this frothy costume drama with melancholy undertones may not have been one of Renoir's masterpieces, but it has his customary offhanded elegance and brio, and a charming performance by Ingrid Bergman, this time beautifully gowned, and it set us up in an infectiously amorous mood.

Another felicitous outcome happened when I took a woman I was just starting to date, Liz, to see Michael Powell's *I Know Where I'm Going*. There is no resisting this cheerful, life-affirming, incurably romantic picture. We remained an item for several years. I was finally learning my lesson: Stay away from crucified lovers and saints burned at the stake. Yet several years into our relationship I took Liz to see a film by the left-wing German filmmaker Alexander Kluge at Anthology Film Archives. It was probably *The Artist in the Circus Dome: Clueless*. Curious about the genre of essay films, I needed to fill in my Kluge gap. We sat watching ninety minutes of assaultive, agitprop, collaged bits, our necks punitively strained in the flat, untilted screening room, and at the end of it she said, "Don't ever take me to a movie like that again."

Eventually I left bachelorhood and married Cheryl, who is properly appreciative of Mizoguchi's *Ugetsu* and a good sport, tolerating my obscurantist tastes. One of the advantages of a long-lasting marriage is that you don't have to woo one's spouse on a movie date with just the right choice. I did not hesitate to take her to Aleksey German's *Hard to Be a God*, for instance. I had seen German's earlier movies, including the brilliant, albeit difficult, *Khrustalyov, My Car!*, and thought him a filmmaking giant, so I was prepared for an otherworldly experience. *Hard to Be a God* was his last picture, which he worked on for years without being able to finish it, a brutal dystopian-medieval epic. I won't lie, it was grueling to sit through, but it had its bleak rewards, and Cheryl was excited to have seen it, as was I. In any case, the stakes were lowered: By this time we could agree or disagree about many more important topics than movie love.

Experience Necessary

There is nothing so beautiful and legitimate as to play the man well and properly, no knowledge so hard to acquire as the knowledge of how to live this life well and naturally; and the most barbarous of our maladies is to despise our being.

—MICHEL DE MONTAIGNE, "Of Experience"

I.

"OF EXPERIENCE" is Montaigne's last and, I insist, greatest essay. It inspires us with its wisdom and balance. Montaigne, like Goethe, had the knack—some would say the bad taste—of benefiting from his experience at every stage of life and achieving a calm, benign perspective with age. Which I can't entirely seem to do. I have reached and passed my seventieth birthday: threescore and ten, the alleged fulfillment of a life span. I am still agitated, perplexed. I look back at all that has happened to me and it seems as though it were practically nothing. To quote the last line of Jorge Luis Borges's poem on Emerson: "I have not lived. I want to be someone else."

2.

On the other hand, I want to be only myself. I think I know what I am about, am comfortable with that person, can distinguish good writing from bad and decent human beings from jerks. Less and less do I feel the need to justify my conclusions. I carry myself in public with impervious self-confidence. (In private is another story.) My students look to me for answers, and I improvise—something that passes for adequate. Most of the dilemmas that shake these young people, their existential, religious, or romantic doubts, their future professional prospects, their worries that someone won't like them, roll off my back. It could be that I am just numbed, unable to summon the urgency behind what to them constitutes a crisis. Mine is the questionable wisdom of passivity. What I cannot change, I no longer let myself be insanely bothered by. Even the latest political folly elicits from me only a disgruntled shrug. I am more upset when my favorite sports team loses, but then I remind myself that it wasn't, technically, my fault since I lacked magical powers to alter the outcome.

3.

"Are you experienced?" asked Jimi Hendrix, tauntingly. Does he mean: Have I slept with fifty groupies, humped a guitar onstage before adulating thousands, taken so many drugs that I risked dying from an overdose? In that sense, no, I am not experienced.

4.

Otherwise, are you experienced? Hell, yes. I know the score. I wasn't born yesterday. I've been around the block a few times. I can tell which way is up. You can't pull a fast one on me. You can't pull the wool over my eyes. I'm from Missouri: Show me. I know a thing or two. I know which side my bread is buttered on. I'm hip. I'm sadder but wiser. I'm no fool. I have eyes in the back of my head. I can tell my left from my right. I know my ass from my elbow. I can see which way the wind blows. I have a pretty good idea. I've been through the mill. I've been around the world in a plane. I've seen it all. *Now* I've seen it all.

5.

"Detachment … is one of the forms that engagement with experience can take: things seen at a remove, appearing strange and so more clearly seen," writes the art historian Svetlana Alpers. Experience can mean plunging into dangerous war zones, witnessing tragedies under fire, like George Orwell at the Spanish front and Susan Sontag in Bosnia, or it can mean staying on the sidelines, exercising watchful prudence. Then there is the experience of ordinary humdrum life, what Virginia Woolf calls cotton wool, those moments of "nonbeing." Bring it on. As Bartleby might say, I prefer not to live at the highest pitch. I have always been a fan of bemused detachment. I am rather attached to the notion of detachment. I accept in advance the guilt for being detached, should any such guilt attach.

6.

"Of Experience" was, as I said, Montaigne's last essay. I wonder if this will be my last essay. I am running out of things to say. Moreover, I feel I have done my life's work as a writer. I have nothing more to prove. It is strange to have come to such a pass and be surrounded by friends and colleagues still pressing on, unsure whether they will have time enough to fulfill their appointed destinies. I have fulfilled a modest destiny modestly. I have done what I set out to do, and now linger on past my assignment. I can still visit museums and relish new movies or old books, can still enjoy a walk through unfamiliar parts of the city, can still participate in the delights, follies, and chagrins of family life, can still teach the young and hold forth in Association of Writing Programs panel discussions, but I don't want to work so hard at writing anymore. It's as if I have a form of post-traumatic stress disorder: all those years trying to meet the challenge of writing well have left me trembling, with a desire for peace and inactivity.

7.

There is an abundance of things I can't do now, and so probably will never do. I can't change a tire to save my life (although if it were a matter of life and death perhaps I could). I can't read sheet music or play the piano. I used to be able to read Hebrew but now I can't without committing lots of errors. I am a poor swimmer and can barely stay alive in the water. I don't run marathons, not because I couldn't, physically speaking, but because I can't *make* myself run a marathon. What I can't do and what I don't care to do are connected at the hip. I don't know Latin. I can't tell one tree or flowering shrub from another. I am at a loss as to how to identify the stars; in fact, my grasp of astronomy is so scant that I could say, with Charles Lamb, "I guess at Venus only by her brightness—and if the sun on some portentous morn were to make his first appearance in the

West, I verily believe, that, while all the world were gasping in apprehension about me, I alone should stand unterrified, from sheer incuriosity and want of observation." My understanding of the way things work, including the laws of physics, is so pathetic it's a wonder I can navigate the world at all. I specialize in ignorance. "What *do* I know?" as Michel would say. It looks as though I won't have sex with a man in this lifetime. Experience has taught me to honor my indifference and my cowardice both. Put it this way: Experience has finally proved to be a school that trains me to limit my concerns and tolerate my limitations.

8.

One privilege of growing older is that you do not have to adjust to the new, or even wax excited about it. I remain a man of the twentieth century. Reluctantly dragged into the new millennium, I stay loyal to the previous one, hewing to the patterns I established then. For instance, I still read the print versions of newspapers and magazines, and dress respectably when I take an airplane. I avoid thinking about Facebook, Twitter, or texting or any such innovations—not that I deplore them, I have no high-minded objections to the new technology, I simply refuse to engage mentally with it. When I happen to glance at op-ed essays about the evolutionary danger these new forms of communication pose to humanist values, I stop reading the article forthwith, because I don't want to care enough about the phenomena even to be alarmed by them. I refuse to be topical. I am thus spared much wasted effort trying to write ingenious think pieces about the latest splash or gizmo.

Experience has also taught me to recognize that much of what passes for innovation is simply puffery, the product of public relations and short memories. In pop or high culture, the "edgy" turns out usually to be the recycling of a tired trope. Take androgyny: Marlene Dietrich wore her tux and kissed a woman on the lips; now Madonna or Lady Gaga does the same. Similarly S/M and black leather, fragmentation, jettisoning of narrative, scrambling of chronology, self-reflexive loops, Artaudian stage ritual, Khlebnikovian nonsense syllables, neo-Dadaist anti-art, Brechtian-Marxist alienation effects, and politically correct consciousness-raising of all stripes.

In my youth, I would read the pages of the *New York Times* Arts & Leisure section (it was called something different then, but no matter) with avid credulity, thinking I must make it a point to catch up with this filmmaker, painter, opera conductor, or theater production. Now I scan the bylines, and knowing most of these arts journalists, whose opinions I don't particularly trust nor do I value their prose styles, hardworking though they may be, I spend more time musing about how they got the assignment than reading through their articles. Does that sound merely snotty or qualify as a sign of experience?

9.

I have experienced enough in the way of people's strange behaviors to not be surprised by sudden breakouts of kindness, brutality, tenderness, betrayal, inconsistency, vanity, rigidity, schadenfreude and its opposite. What does surprise me is current events. When 9/11 happened I was taken aback by such a freakish thing. (It was, to me, no accident that 9/11 occurred on the other side of the millennium, in 2001: No good, I thought, can come of the twenty-first century. Not that the twentieth did not have its share of nasty surprises.) I continue to marvel at Republicans' seeming willingness to shut down the federal government and allow the United States to default rather than negotiate with the president. I don't understand my country anymore: how, after a century of federal programs such as the New Deal, social security, bank regulation, public housing, and food stamps, a large swath of the population can still take umbrage at the government's minimal efforts to protect the weak and the poor, or indeed to have a presence in any aspect of life beyond the maintenance of a military force. Nothing prior has prepared me for this frightening swerve. I grew up in the postwar atmosphere of a modestly progressive welfare state, where problems such as racial segregation and poverty were expected to be addressed at the governmental level, and I assumed naively that we were marching at best or creeping at worst toward a more just society. What I took for an inevitable historical progression turned out to be an anomalous blip. I might better have looked to Nietzsche's theory of eternal recurrence. Today I am less experienced, less able to adapt to this harshly selfish environment than the average twenty-year-old, who has grown up without my New Deal–Great Society set of expectations.

10.

Newspapers were once enormously important; now they're not. I am a creature of newspaper culture, therefore I'm no longer important. I'm redundant. I must learn to accept my redundancy, like Ivan

Turgenev's superfluous man. Fortunately, I've had plenty of practice.
I always anticipated I would be redundant, a cultural throwback,
which is why I prepared by steeping myself in the antiquarian tomes
of ages past, whose authors' names I suspected would mean next to
nothing to future generations. When my writer friends in college
were reading Samuel Beckett, William Burroughs, and Thomas
Pynchon, I was poring over Henry Fielding, Machado de Assis, and
Lady Murasaki. Later, when I discovered the joys of the personal
essay, I clung to the fustian charms of Charles Lamb, William
Hazlitt, Robert Louis Stevenson, and Max Beerbohm, with scarcely
a side-glance at David Sedaris, David Foster Wallace, or Sarah Vow-
ell. I have cheerfully morphed into the type whose idea of a fun
movie, as my teenage daughter scoffingly reminds me, is a restored
black-and-white silent film.

So what good is experience if the experience I have managed to
acquire no longer applies to the new era's challenges, except as the
contrarian stiffening of my stubbornness in the face of novelty, and
the embrace of the antedated and rarefied?

II.

Emerson rebukes me:

> But the man and woman of seventy assume to know all, they have
> outlived their hope, they renounce aspiration, accept the actual for
> the necessary, and talk down to the young. Let them, then, become
> organs of the Holy Ghost; let them be lovers; let them behold
> truth; and their eyes are uplifted, their wrinkles smoothed, they are

perfumed again with hope and power. This old age ought not to creep on a human mind. In nature every moment is new; the past is always swallowed and forgotten; the coming only is sacred. Nothing is secure but life, transition, the energizing spirit.... People wish to be settled; only as far as they are unsettled is there any hope for them.

Yeah, yeah, so you say. I *do* wish to be settled; perhaps I *have* outlived my hope. When Emerson wrote this passage it must have sounded fresh, rebellious, positively electric. Now it sounds dated. I realize that even in choosing to let Ralph Waldo Emerson rebuke me, I am indulging in an antiquarian longing.

12.

These are the last six lines of that beautiful Borges poem about Emerson:

> He thinks: I have read the essential books
> And written others which oblivion
> Will not efface. I have been allowed
> That which is given mortal man to know.
> The whole continent knows my name.
> I have not lived. I want to be someone else.

Well, the whole continent does not know my name, but I am ... respected. I have read a good many essential books (alas, forgetting most of what was in them, so that I find I have to read them again from scratch) and have written more than a dozen books which, if not guaranteed to escape oblivion, have given some pleasure to some readers. More than that I will not, must not ask: the gods get angry at ingratitude. I am not grandiose enough, like Emerson or Borges, to think it even my place to want to be someone else. (This reminds me of the old Jewish joke: The rabbi and the synagogue bigwigs are beating their breasts on Yom Kippur, the Day of Atonement, and crying out, "I'm a worm, I'm nothing, I'm nobody." The janitor, a goy, decides it looks like a good idea, and starts beating his chest too and moaning, "I'm nobody, I'm nobody!" They stare at him with alarmed disdain, until one of them says, "Look who thinks he's Nobody!") Is it faux naive and presumptuous to consider myself a nobody, a mere minute speck under the stars, or is the larger geological perspective of looming environmental catastrophe the only proper and responsible one?

13.

What is the nature of experience? What is the connection, if any, between experience and knowledge? What is the relationship between knowledge and wisdom? Can one acquire wisdom passively? Can one live and *not* acquire experience? Is experience only "experience" if it has been converted into self-conscious thought, or do we count the unconscious in our stock of experience? Our dreams, for instance: are they not part of our experience? By the way, is there really such a thing as the unconscious? Is wisdom principally an intellectual or an emotional property? Can wisdom bypass the heart and lodge only in the brain? Or does it ever work vice versa? What is the difference in value between a shady experience consciously undertaken and one prudently avoided? Does prudence, meaning the wise avoidance of certain sketchy paths, result in a shallower or a deeper soul? Is there even such a thing as the soul? If not, what is the point of gaining experience?

14.

We are great fools. "He has spent his life in idleness," we say; "I have done nothing today." What, have you not lived? That is not only the fundamental but the most illustrious of your occupations. "If I had been placed in a position to manage great affairs, I would have shown what I could do." Have you been able to think out and manage your own life? You have done the greatest task of all. . . . To compose our character is our duty, not to compose books, and to win, not battles and provinces, but order and tranquility in our conduct. Our great and glorious masterpiece is to live appropriately.

So said Montaigne, who wrote "Of Experience" at fifty-six, and died when he was fifty-nine. We'll say sixty, for the sake of round numbers. Since seventy is the new sixty, I should be reaching that point of ripe wisdom that Montaigne attained at the end of his life, no? But since the average young person today has so protracted an adolescence, compared to a youth in sixteenth-century France (see Philippe Ariès's *Centuries of Childhood*, which demonstrated that children were treated as little adults and expected to work from age seven on), we would have to subtract an additional twenty years from my maturity index, bringing me down to age forty. Then take another ten years off for the syndrome that Ernest Hemingway contemptuously called the "American boy-man," meaning that there was something uniquely arrested-development about the males in this particular land, which would reduce my emotional age even further, so I should probably be considered the equivalent of a thirty-year-old. No wonder I am still blinking my eyes like a hatched chick and pondering what's what.

15.

The problem of solipsism: not believing that others are as real as you are would seem to put a lid on acquiring wisdom. On the other hand, maybe we are all narcissists, and if narcissism proves to be the universal law, then we need to reexamine all the high-minded inveighing against narcissism and ask if it is a hypocritical form of social coercion. Why should we feel guilty about something we cannot avoid?

I don't think I'm really a narcissist of the first order. Unlike Montaigne, I'm not even terribly interested in myself. When I'm alone, in my study or walking the streets, I am usually thinking not about me but about other people, trying to figure them out, though that could just be another form of narcissistic self-protection: trying to anticipate what they might do, so as to parry it effectively when the situation arises. In any case, I am something of a literalist when it comes to reality. I assume that the people around me *are* real, the tree outside my window is real, etc. I have never understood that notion put forward by Jean Baudrillard or David Shields that we less and less feel our lives to be real, that the simulacra incessantly produced by the media have robbed us of the sense of our own authenticity, and therefore we hunger for the real. I don't hunger for the real. I don't have the foggiest notion what that means. I just want to get by, I just want to enjoy what years are left to me on earth, and most of all, I want to watch my daughter, Lily, turn into the amazing adult she is fast becoming, want to watch her embrace her full potential and her destiny. I worry about her fretting too much. Amor fati, I want to tell her. Love your fate—which I also tell myself constantly, for all the good that it does.

16.

I wake up between six and six thirty each morning, having to pee. My cats know this about me and begin to rummage about the bed at that hour, to make sure I will get up and feed them. I put glaucoma-controlling drops in my eyes the first thing in the morning and the last thing at night. I have no problem dropping off to sleep, but I wake up in the night more often than I used to, sometimes roused by noisy neighbors, sometimes by snoring (mine or my wife's), sometimes by a dream, or for no discernible reason whatsoever. I wake up and start picking my nose, to clear the breathing passageways. This is particularly true in winter, when the heat goes on at night and dries out the bedroom air. Because I don't get enough sleep, in the late afternoon I find my eyes drooping when I read, and many times when I am at the movies or listening to an opera I start nodding off. It's outrageous to pay so much for opera tickets and then doze, but I can't help myself. Sometimes, just to keep awake, I rub my scalp above my forehead where there used to be hair, and often find bumps that I try to smooth out by picking off the loose flesh. When I am in a public place such as the subway or at the movies I am always worrying about bedbugs latching on to me, ever since we had an infestation of them a few years back and had to take extreme measures to rid ourselves, hauling all our clothing off to the dry cleaners, and wrapping the books. Every time my skin itches I think it must be bedbugs returning.

17.

I hate to lie, and will do almost anything to avoid telling a lie, even if it means sneaking out of a poetry reading the moment it's over or, if directly accosted, blurting out something undiplomatic and giving offense. This resistance to lying stems not so much from an ethical principle as a superstitious dread, as though if I ever started to lie glibly, my core self would dissolve and I would become a creature of multiple personalities. When you lie you split yourself into two selves, and then a third self has to keep watch and adjudicate the first two. Hence, adultery has never been much of an option for me. Of course I have lied, on some occasions, but I am not going to tell you where or when. *That* experienced I am. Most of my lies are sins of omission, like keeping my mouth shut when I could get in trouble by saying what I actually thought. If someone tells me that he loved a movie I found abysmal, I smile and nod enthusiastically, though with a slight catch of the head, so that if God is watching, He will understand and forgive my deception. Why should we be transparent, though? Is art transparent? Better to honor the mysteries. There is so much we will never be able to understand that we do not need to go in search of mystery, it will come to us regardless.

Coda

In responding to Montaigne's great last essay, I have attempted to
gather my own notions and hunches about experience. I began writing my piece before rereading Montaigne's, telling myself that
I would get a head start in this way; but in the end I could not bring
myself to reread his text carefully—though I skimmed it for under-
lined passages—because it was too depressing. I felt too inadequate
next to his bold, life-embracing manner. He was the master, he was
the Father, and I could not engage him in Oedipal struggle because
I owed him everything as an essayist and knew it. The most I could
do in the way of resisting his domination was to evade rereading his
essay while writing my own. Mind you, I had read "Of Experience"
at least fifteen times, having taught it often over the years, and it was
during one of these readings that I came to the definitive conclusion
that it was his best, so much so that I second-guessed myself for
including "On Some Verses of Virgil," his sexual meditation that
I hoped would be popular with young readers, in my anthology *The
Art of the Personal Essay*, instead of his more conclusive one on
experience.

This was my third attempt to use Montaigne self-consciously as
an influence. I had tried to appropriate his aphoristic manner in my
essay "Against Joie de Vivre," and his listing of anatomical quirks in
"Portrait of My Body." But when it came to approximating his robust
final summations on life experience, I could not. I found my own
grasp on experience much more tentative. And here we come to my
apprehensions about the unitary self. I have been maintaining for
quite a while that personal essayists assert a cohesive self and, in this
respect, are more traditional than the postmodernists or French
theorists who question the whole idea of the individual self. Now

the fact is that I don't know whether my self is unitary, cohesive, or even that it exists—only that it profits me in my essay-writing to proceed according to the assumption that it is. I *pretend* that I have a unitary self, and that is good enough to get me started. Montaigne, for all his proclamations about doubt and the ever-changeable, undulating inconstancy of the human animal, does have, it seems to me, a single, self-confident, fracture-proof self. Or maybe it is his voice that seems so all of a piece to me. He manages to sustain that self, that dryly mellifluous voice, through lengthy essays that digress and return to the main matter over and over. I, on the other hand, could only sustain an essay on experience that came to fewer than twenty pages by breaking it into seventeen measly sections. I did the mosaic thing, wrote it in fragments with space breaks surrounding each discontinuous piece, which is not the way I usually compose essays. Usually I get up a good head of steam and follow it to the end. But I found myself fragmenting in the face of the Gascon's cliff-like certitude. Actually, what brought him to his nobly stoical awareness that "We must learn to endure what we cannot avoid," and what held together that last essay of his was his kidney stones. That disease was the central teacher of his final years: "But is there anything so sweet as that sudden change, when from extreme pain, by the voiding of my stone, I come to recover as if by lightning the beautiful light of health, so free and so full, as happens in our sudden and sharpest attacks of colic?" No thanks. I will take my prolonged, unresolved immaturity over his enlightenment via kidney stones.

PHILLIP LOPATE is the author of the essay collections *Against Joie de Vivre*, *Bachelorhood*, *Being with Children*, *Portrait of My Body*, and *Totally, Tenderly, Tragically*; and of the novels *The Rug Merchant* and *Confessions of a Summer*. He has edited the anthologies *The Art of the Personal Essay*, *The Glorious American Essay*, *The Golden Age of the American Essay*, and *The Contemporary American Essay*. His most recent books are *Portrait Inside My Head*, *To Show and to Tell*, and *A Mother's Tale*.